METAVERSE

Everything you Need to Know about the Future of Decentralized Finance (DeFi), Blockchain Gaming, NFT (Non Fungible Token) and Cryptocurrency

Lucas Peters

© Copyright 2021 by Lucas Peters
All rights reserved.

This document's goal is to provide accurate and trustworthy information on the topic and subject at hand. The book is purchased to understand that the publisher is under no obligation to provide accounting, legal, or other qualified services. If legal or professional counsel is required, a well-versed specialist should be consulted.

A Committee of the American Bar Association and a Committee of Publishers and Associations recognized and approved the Declaration of Principles.

No part of this publication may be reproduced, duplicated, or transmitted in any form, whether electronic or printed. It is strictly forbidden to record this publication, and any storing of this material is only permitted with the publisher's prior consent. All intellectual property rights are reserved.

The data shown here is said to be accurate and consistent. Any liability arising from the use or misuse of any policies, processes, or directions included here, whether due to inattention or otherwise, is solely and completely the responsibility of the receiving reader. The publisher will not be held liable for any compensation, damages, or monetary loss experienced due to the information contained herein, whether directly or indirectly.

All copyrights not held by the publisher belong to the authors.

Because the information offered here is simply for educational purposes, it is universal. The information is provided without any kind of contract or commitment.

The trademarks are utilized without the trademark owner's permission or support, and the trademark is published without the trademark owner's approval or support. All trademarks and brands referenced in this book belong to their respective owners and have no connection to this publication.

Table of Contents

INTRODUCTION 6

CHAPTER 1: 11

WHAT DOES 'METAVERSE' REALLY MEAN? 11

CHAPTER 2: 21

WHY DOES IT MATTER?... 21

CHAPTER 3: 40

WHO ELSE CAN BUILD THE METAVERSE? 40

CHAPTER 4: 67

WHAT'S THE METAVERSE LIKE RIGHT NOW?.... 67

CHAPTER 5: 77

FUTURE OF THE METAVERSE ECONOMY 77

CHAPTER 6: 87

AUGMENTED REALITY (AR) 87

CHAPTER 7: 102

THE INVESTMENT OF NTF'S IN THE
METAVERSE 102

CHAPTER 8: 119

MARKETING IN THE METAVERSE 119

CHAPTER 9: 125

TOP METAVERSE INVESTMENTS TO
SKYROCKET 125
CHAPTER 10: 139
HOW METAVERSE IS EVOLVING DIGITAL
WORLD? 139
CHAPTER 11: 146
METAVERSE: THE EVOLUTION OF A NOVEL
TECHNOLOGY AND WHAT IT MEANS FOR THE
FUTURE 146
CONCLUSION 152

INTRODUCTION

Technology often delivers unexpected outcomes that no one foresees. On the other hand, the most significant advances were frequently predicted decades ago. Vannevar Bush proposed the "Memex" in 1945, a single device that would hold all books, records, and communications and mechanically connect them by association. This idea was then utilized to construct the concept of "hypertext" (a term coined two decades later), which aided the development of the World Wide Web (developed another two decades later). Although the "Streaming Wars" has only recently begun, the first streaming video was broadcast more than 25 years ago. Many of the characteristics of this so-called war, such as essentially endless supplies of content, interactivity, dynamic and targeted marketing, on-demand playback, and the benefit of combining content and delivery, have been speculated about for decades.

In this way, the broad contours of future solutions are frequently anticipated and, in some ways, decided upon well before the technical competence to generate them. Still, it's difficult to foresee how they'll come together, whose characteristics will matter more or less, what governance models or competitive dynamics will drive them, or what new experiences will emerge. Much of Hollywood recognized that the future of television was online when Netflix started its streaming service (IP TV had been deployed in the late 1999s). The issue was timing and how to package such a service (Hollywood required another ten years to realize that all its channels, genres, and content needed to be consolidated into a single app/brand). Many in the media industry are still baffled by the popularity of video game broadcasting and YouTubers and the notion that the best way to commercialize material is to give it out for free and charge $0.99 for optional $0.99 things of no consequence. The acquisition of media conglomerate Time Warner by landline internet behemoth AOL was announced in 2000 to bring media and technology/distribution closer together, but it was abandoned in 2009 after failing to deliver many benefits. Nine years later, it was then purchased under the same premise by AT&T, the mobile internet behemoth.

While many technologists anticipated a "personal computer," its attributes and timing were so unpredictably unexpected that Microsoft, rather than IBM, dominated the PC era in the 1990s. While Microsoft anticipated mobile, it misjudged the operating system and hardware role, resulting in the global rise of Android and iOS (and Microsoft's shift from the OS layer to the app/services layer). Similarly, Steve Jobs' computing goals were always "right," but they were established too early and on the wrong device. Email and instant messaging were the two most popular uses of the early Internet, but it wasn't until the late 2000s that the value of social apps/networks was acknowledged. Similarly, all of the conditions for creating Facebook existed before to the year 2000; however, Facebook did not arrive until 2005 - and even then, it was by chance.

Many in the technology community have imagined a future state of the Internet, if not a quasi-successor to it, called the "Metaverse," since the late 1970s and early

1980s. It would transform not only the digital world's infrastructure but also much of the physical world, as well as all the platforms and services that sit on top of it, how they work, and what they sell. Although the Metaverse's full vision is difficult to define, appears unbelievable, and is decades away, the pieces have begun to feel very real. And, as is customary with this type of change, the journey is as long and unpredictable as the payoff.

As a result, several of the world's tech behemoths have made the Metaverse their newest macro-goal. Epic Games, the creators of the Unreal Engine and Fortnite, has made it their explicit goal, as I stated in February of this year. It's also the driving force behind Facebook's acquisition of Oculus VR and the recently announced Horizon virtual world/meeting space, as well as a slew of other initiatives, including AR glasses and brain-to-machine interfaces and communication. Similarly, the tens of billions of dollars that will be spent on cloud gaming over the next decade are based on the belief that such technologies will underpin our online-offline virtual future.

Many of the same objects may be seen in the offices of Big Tech CEOs. However, a copy of Neal Stephenson's Snow Crash, which first described and essentially coined "Metaverse" and "Avatar," is likely to be the most well-worn. There are numerous explanations for this.

Debating the meaning of "the metaverse" is akin to debating the meaning of "the internet" in the 1970s.

The framework for a new way of communication was being laid, but no one knew what the finished product would look like. While it was true that "the internet" was on the way at the time, not every image of what it would include was accurate.

On the other hand, the metaverse concept is surrounded by a lot of marketing hype. Facebook, in particular, is in a vulnerable position due to Apple's decision to limit ad tracking, which has hurt the company's financial line. It is impossible to separate Facebook's vision of a future in which everyone has a digital wardrobe to browse because the company intends to profit from selling virtual garments.

Chapter 1:

WHAT DOES 'METAVERSE' REALLY MEAN?

Here's an experiment to demonstrate how ambiguous and perplexing the phrase "metaverse" may be: Replace the phrase "the metaverse" with "cyberspace" in a sentence. The meaning will not change 90% of the time. Rather than referring to a specific type of technology, the word alludes to a wide shift in how we interact with it. It's highly possible that the term will become obsolete even if the technology it initially defined becomes widespread.

The metaverse is made up of two technologies: virtual reality, which is distinguished by persistent virtual settings that exist even when you are not playing, and augmented reality, which combines physical and digital world features. However, it does not necessitate that those areas be only accessible through VR or AR. A virtual environment accessible through PCs, game consoles, and even phones, such as Fortnite, might be metaversal.

It also refers to a digital economy where users can design, buy, and sell products. It's also interoperable, allowing you to transport virtual things like clothing or vehicles from one platform to another in more idealized metaverse scenarios. You may buy a shirt in the mall and then wear it to the movies in real life. Virtual identities, avatars, and inventories are already confined to a single platform on most platforms, but a metaverse might allow you to create a persona that you can carry with you wherever you go as easy as transferring your profile image from one social network to another.

It's difficult to understand what all of this implies since you might say, "Wait, doesn't it already exist?" when you hear descriptions like the ones above. The Environment of Warcraft, for example, is a persistent virtual environment where people can buy and trade things. Rick Sanchez may learn about Martin Luther King Jr. through virtual experiences like concerts and a Fortnite exhibit. You can put on an Oculus headset and enter your virtual world. Is that the definition of "metaverse"? Is it just a few new types of video games?

In a nutshell, yes and no. To call Fortnite "the metaverse" refers to Google as "the internet." Even if you spend a lot of time chatting, buying, learning, and playing games in Fortnite, it doesn't mean you'll learn everything there is to know about the metaverse.

Science fiction is where the most common concepts about the Metaverse originate from. The Metaverse is usually depicted as a kind of digital "jacked-in" internet — a manifestation of true reality but grounded in a virtual (often theme park-like) world, similar to that depicted in Ready Player One and The Matrix. While such experiences are likely to exist in the Metaverse, they are constrained in the same manner that films like Tron portrayed the Internet as a true digital "information superhighway" of bits.

We don't know how to define the Metaverse, just as it was impossible to envisage the Internet of 2020 in 1982 — and much more difficult to express it to people who had never "logged" onto it. On the other hand, core traits can be discovered.

1. Be persistent – That is, it never "resets," "pauses," or "terminates," but rather continues endlessly.

2. Be synchronous and live – while pre-planned and self-contained events will take place, the Metaverse will be a live experience that exists in real-time for everyone, exactly like it happens in "real life."

3. Allow for an infinite number of concurrent users while maintaining each user's sense of "presence" – everyone can be a part of the Metaverse and engage in a certain event/place/activity at the same time and with their agency.

4. Be a fully functional economy — individuals and businesses will be able to create, own, invest, sell, and be compensated for a vast array of "labor" that produces "value" that is valued by others.

5. Be a hybrid of digital and physical worlds, private and public networks/experiences, and open and closed platforms.

6. Provide unprecedented data, digital items/assets, content, and so on interoperability across each of these experiences — for example, your Counter-Strike gun skin might be used to paint a pistol in Fortnite or gifted to a

buddy on/through Facebook. A automobile created for Rocket League (or even Porsche's website) might be carried across to work in Roblox in the same way. Today's digital world functions similarly to a shopping mall, with each store having its own unique ID cards, currency, proprietary units of measurement for commodities such as shoes or calories, and distinct dress codes, among other things.

7. Be inhabited by "content" and "experiences" developed and operated by a vast array of contributors, some of whom are self-employed people, while others may be informally organized organizations or commercially oriented businesses.

8. A few other concepts could be fundamental to the Metaverse, although they aren't universally accepted. One of these concerns is whether individuals would have a single digital identity (or "avatar") to utilize throughout all of their interactions. This might be beneficial, but it's unlikely since each of the leaders of the "Metaverse age" will still require their own identification systems. There are a few main account systems available today, but none of them spans the full web, and they usually stack on top

of one another with restricted data sharing and access (e.g., your iPhone is based around an iOS account, then you might log into an application using your Facebook ID, which itself is your Gmail account).

9. There's also a discussion over how much interoperability is necessary for the Metaverse to genuinely be "the Metaverse," rather than merely an evolution of the Internet as it now exists. Many people also wonder if there can be just one operator in a true Metaverse (as is the case in Ready Player One). Some claim that a Metaverse's definition (and success) requires a strongly decentralized platform built mostly on community-driven standards and protocols (akin to the open web) and a "open source" Metaverse OS or platform (though this doesn't rule out the presence of dominant closed platforms in the Metaverse).

10. The Metaverse's basic communications architecture is another concept. While the Internet today is based on individual servers "talking" to one another as needed, some believe the Metaverse should be "wired" and "managed" around constant many-to-many connections.

There's no consensus on how this would work or the extent of decentralization that would be required.

11. It's also useful to consider what the Metaverse is frequently compared to, albeit wrongly. While these comparisons are most likely a part of the Metaverse, they aren't the Metaverse themselves. The Metaverse, for example, isn't...

A "virtual world" – Virtual worlds and games with AI-driven characters, as well as those populated with "actual" humans in real-time, have existed for decades. This is a synthetic and fictional universe, not a "meta" (Greek for "beyond") universe with a single goal (a game).

1. A "virtual space" – Digital content experiences such as Second Life are frequently referred to as "proto-Metaverses" because they (A) lack game-like goals or skill systems; (B) are persistent virtual hangouts; (C) provide near-synchronous content updates, and (D) feature real people represented by digital avatars. These, however, are insufficient characteristics for the Metaverse.

2. "Virtual reality" (VR) - VR is a method of immersing oneself in a virtual environment or area. A sense of presence in a digital world is not enough to constitute a

Metaverse. It's the same as claiming to live in a prosperous metropolis because you can see and walk about it.

3. A "digital and virtual economy" - Too, is already in place. Like World of Warcraft, individual games have had functional economies for a long time, where real individuals trade virtual products for real money or do virtual jobs for real money. Furthermore, platforms like Amazon's Mechanical Turk and technology like Bitcoin are built on the employment of individuals/businesses/computing power to complete virtual and digital work. We are already trading at scale through purely digital marketplaces for purely digital things for purely digital activities.

4. A "game" - Fortnite contains numerous Metaverse elements. It (A) mashes up IP; (B) has a consistent identity that spans many closed platforms; (C) is a portal to a diverse range of experiences, some of which are entirely social; and (D) rewards content creators, among other things. However, like with Ready Player One, it remains too limited in terms of what it can do, how far it can go, and what "work" can be done (at least for now). While the Metaverse may have some game-like aims, feature

games, and use gamification, it isn't a game in and of itself, nor is it focused on specific goals.

5. A "virtual Disneyland or theme park" – Not only will there be an endless number of "attractions," but they will also not be "planned" or "programmed" in the same way that Disneyland is, nor will they all be about fun or entertainment. Furthermore, the engagement distribution will have a very long tail.

6. There will be a "new app store" – Nobody needs a new means to access apps, and doing so "in VR" (for example) would not unlock/enable the kinds of value promised by a successor Internet. The Metaverse differs significantly from today's Internet/mobile architecture, paradigms, and objectives.

7. A "new UGC platform" — The Metaverse isn't just another YouTube or Facebook-like platform where countless people can "produce," "share," and "monetize" content, with the most popular content accounting for only a small portion of total consumption. The Metaverse will be a location where proper empires are established and where these well-capitalized corporations may fully own a consumer, control APIs/data, and unit economics,

among other things. Furthermore, like with the web, a dozen or so platforms likely control a major portion of user time, experiences, content, and so on.

(In other words, think of the Metaverse as the Nightmare Before Christmas - you can walk into any event or activity and potentially fulfill practically any of your needs, from a single starting point or planet populated by everyone you know.) This is why hypertext is so important. However, it's critical to understand that the Metaverse is not a game, a piece of technology, or an online experience. It's the equivalent of claiming that World of Warcraft, the iPhone, or Google is the Internet. They include digital environments, devices, services, and websites, among other things. The Internet is made up of a variety of protocols, technology, tubes, and languages and access devices, information, and communication experiences. The Metaverse will be as well.)

Chapter 2:

WHY DOES IT MATTER?

Even if the Metaverse falls short of the extravagant expectations of science fiction authors, it is predicted to create trillions of dollars in value as a new computer platform or content medium. The Metaverse, in its final form, serves as a gateway to most digital experiences, as well as a crucial component of all physical ones and the next major labor platform.

The advantage of being a significant player in such a system is self-evident — the Internet has no "owner," but virtually all of the largest Internet enterprises are among the top ten most valuable public companies in the world. There will undoubtedly be far greater economic benefits if the Metaverse acts as a functional "successor" to the web, with far more reach, time spent, and commercial activity. Regardless, the Metaverse should provide the same range of opportunities as the web, with new companies, products, and services handling everything from payment processing to identity verification, hiring, ad distribution, content production, and security, among other things. As a result, several incumbents are likely to lose their seats.

In general, the Metaverse has the potential to change how we allocate and commercialize modern resources. Developed economies have changed for centuries as labor, and real estate scarcity swelled and waned. Would-be laborers living outside of cities will engage in the "high value" economy through virtual labor in the Metaverse. We will see further alterations in where we live, the infrastructure created, and who performs specific duties as more consumer expenses goes to virtual goods, services, and experiences. Consider the concept of "Gold Farming." Many "players" – often employed by a larger corporation and often from lower-income nations – would spend a workday gathering digital resources for sale outside or inside the game not long after in-game trade economies formed. In the West, these sales were typical to higher-income players. While most "labor" is menial, repetitive, and limited to a few applications, the variety and value of this "work" will expand in tandem with the Metaverse.

BUILDING THE METAVERSE

The Metaverse will necessitate a plethora of new technologies, protocols, enterprises, breakthroughs, and discoveries to function. And it won't appear out of nowhere; there won't be a clear "Before Metaverse" and "After Metaverse" distinction. Rather, it will emerge gradually over time as various goods, services, and capabilities connect and meld. However, it's useful to consider three key factors that must be in place.

(One way I try to think about these three categories procedurally is through the Book of Genesis - first, establish the underlying universe ("concurrency infrastructure"), then describe its laws of physics and regulations ("standards and protocols"), and finally, one must fill it with worthwhile content ("Content") that evolves and iterates against selection pressures. In other words, God does not make and design the universe as if it were a small model, but rather allows one to expand across a mostly empty tableau, etc.)

Concurrency Infrastructure

At its most fundamental level, the technology does not yet exist to support hundreds, much alone millions, of individuals sharing a synchronized experience. Consider the Marshmello concert in Fortnite in 2019. 11 million people in total watched the event in real-time. They did not, however, do so in tandem. In reality, there were over 100,000 Marshmello concert instances, each of which was slightly out of rhythm and limited to 100 players. Epic can certainly handle more today, but not into the hundreds of thousands, let alone millions.

Not only does the Metaverse necessitate infrastructure that does not already exist, but the Internet was never designed for anything remotely similar to this. It was, after all, created to transfer files from one machine to another. So, most of the Internet's underlying systems are based on a single server communicating with another server or an end-user device. This model is still in use today. Although billions of individuals are on today's Facebook, each user has their connection to the Facebook server and does not share it with anybody else. As a result, when you access content from another user, you're just getting the most up-to-date information from Facebook. Text conversations were the first pseudo-synchronous applications, but you're still feeding primarily static data to a server and pulling the most up-to-date data from it when/where/how/as needed. The Internet was never intended for persistent (as opposed to continuous) communication, let alone persistent communication synchronized in real time with many other people.

The Metaverse requires something more akin to video games and video conferencing to function. These encounters operate because of persistent connections that keep each other up to date in real-time and with a level of precision that other programs don't require. However, they rarely have a large number of concurrent users: most video chat systems have a limit of a few individuals, and after you reach 50, you'll have to "live stream" a broadcast to your viewers instead of sharing a two-way connection. These encounters don't have to be real, and they certainly aren't.

To that end, one of the reasons the battle royale genre has only lately been popular in video games is that it is only now possible to play live with so many other players. Although some of the most popular games, such as

Second Life and Warcraft, have been around for more than two decades, they essentially faked the experience by "sharding" and dividing gamers into distinct "worlds" and servers. For example, Eve Online can have over 100,000 players "in the same game," although they are spread across multiple universes (i.e., server nodes). As a result, a player only sees or interacts with a small number of other players at any given time. Furthermore, getting to another galaxy necessitates quitting from one server and loading another (which the game manages to "conceal" narratively by forcing players to travel at light speed to span the immensity of space). And if/when Eve Online reached battles with hundreds of players, the system ground to a halt. And it worked because the game's gameplay dynamic was primarily built on large-scale, pre-planned ship-based conflict. These slowdowns

It would have rendered the game unplayable if it had been a "fast-twitch" game like Rocket League or Call of Duty.

Like the appropriately called Improbable, several companies are working hard to overcome this challenge.

However, this massive computational issue goes against the Internet's core design/intent.

Standards, Protocols, and their Adoption

Standards and protocols for visual presentation, communications, graphics, file loading, data, and so on make the Internet work as we know it today. This includes everything from well-known brands to obscure ones. The WebSocket protocol, which underpins almost every form of real-time communication between a browser and other servers on the internet, assigns GIF filetypes to it.

S&Ps will need to be even broader, more complex, and resilient in the Metaverse. Furthermore, because interoperability and live synchronous experiences are important, we'll have to prune some existing standards and "standardize" around a smaller set of standards per function—for example, today's image file formats include.GIF,.JPEG,.PNG,.BMP, TIFF, WEBP, and others. Even though today's web is based on open standards, much of it is closed and proprietary. Amazon, Facebook, and Google all use similar technologies, but they're not designed to work together in the same way that Ford's wheels aren't designed to fit into a GM chassis.

Furthermore, these businesses are adamant about not integrating their systems or sharing their data. Such actions may increase the "digital economy's" overall value, but they also weaken their hyper-valuable network effects, making it easier for users to move their digital lives elsewhere.

This will be extremely difficult and time-consuming. The more valuable and interoperable the Metaverse becomes, the more difficult it will be to reach an industry-wide agreement on issues like data security, data persistence, forward-compatible code evolution, and transactions. Furthermore, the Metaverse will require entirely new rules for censorship, communication control, regulatory enforcement, tax reporting, the prevention of online radicalization, and a slew of other issues with which we're still grappling today.

While standard-setting usually entails face-to-face meetings, negotiations, and debates, the Metaverse's standards will not be established in advance. Meetings and opinions change on an ad hoc basis in the standard process, which is much messier and more organic.

Consider SimCity as a meta parallel for the Metaverse. Ideally, the "Mayor" (i.e., player) would design their mega-metropolis first, then construct it from the ground up. However, you cannot simply "create" a 10MM person metropolis in the game, as you cannot in real life. You begin by focusing on a tiny town and optimizing it (e.g., where the roads are, schools are, utility capacity, etc.). You build around this town as it grows, occasionally but prudently demolishing and replacing "old" areas, sometimes only if/when a problem (lack of power) or calamity strikes (a fire). However, unlike SimCity, there will be multiple mayors rather than just one, and their ambitions and incentives will frequently clash.

We do not know exactly what the Metaverse will require, much less how, when, or through which applications and groups existing standards will be transferred. As a result, it's crucial to evaluate how the Metaverse develops rather than just the technology standard it follows.

The 'On-Ramp' Experience
Consumers and businesses will not adopt a would-be proto-Metaverse simply because it is offered, just as Metaverse standards cannot be "announced."

Take a look at reality. Making a mall large enough to accommodate a hundred thousand people or a hundred stores does not guarantee to attract a single customer or brand. To meet current civilian and commercial demands, "town squares" form spontaneously around existing infrastructure and activities. In the end, any gathering spot — whether it's a bar, basement, park, museum, or merry-go-round — is visited because of who or what is already present, not because it's a destination in and of itself.

The same can be said for digital encounters. Facebook, the world's largest social network, succeeded not because it declared itself a "social network," but rather because it began as a college hot-or-not, evolved into a digital yearbook, and became a photo-sharing messaging service. The Metaverse, like Facebook, must be "populated," not simply "populate," and this population must then fill up the gaps in this digital environment with activities to do and stuff to consume.

This is why thinking about Fortnite as a video game, or an interactive experience is too limited and too quick. Fortnite began as a game, but it swiftly morphed into a social media platform. From the 1970s until the 2010s, teenagers would come home and speak on the phone for three hours. They now chat about Fortnite with their buddies, but not about Fortnite. Instead, they discuss school, movies, sports, the news, boys and girls, and other topics. After all, Fortnite does not have a story or an IP; the plot revolves around what happens on the island and who is present.

In addition, Fortnite is quickly becoming a platform for other businesses, IP, and stories to express themselves. This includes, most notably, last year's live Marshmello show. However, since then, the number of similar examples has exploded. In December 2019, as part of a larger in-game audience-interactive event that included a live mocap interview with director J.J. Abrams, Star Wars: The Rise of Skywalker released a clip from the highly anticipated film only in Fortnite. Furthermore, this event was mentioned openly in the film's opening scenes. Weezer created a special island where fans may get an early listen to their new album (while dancing with other "players"). In addition, Fortnite has created various themed "limited-time modes" based on Nike's Air Jordan and Lionsgate's John Wick film franchise. In other situations, these "LTMs" turn a section of the Fortnite map into a mini-virtual world that, when accessed, modifies the game's visuals, items, and playstyle to mimic something else. This has included the Borderlands universe, Gotham, Batman's hometown, and the old west.

As a result, Fortnite is one of the few locations where Marvel and DC's IP collide. You may practically dress up like a Marvel character and converse with others wearing officially approved NFL uniforms in Gotham City. This is the first time something like this has happened. It will, nevertheless, be crucial to the Metaverse.

More broadly, Fortnite has spawned a new sub-economy where "players" can create (and monetize) their content. Digital clothing ("skins") or dances ("emotes") are examples of this. It has, however, quickly grown to include all new games and experiences that use Fortnite's engine, assets, and aesthetics. From basic treasure hunts to immersive mash-ups of the Brothers Grimm with parkour culture to a 10-hour sci-fi epic spanning several realms and timelines, there's something for everyone. Fortnite's Creative Mode, in fact, already feels like a pre-Metaverse. A player enters a game-like lobby and selects from thousands of "doors" (i.e., space-time rifts) that transport them to one of the thousands of distinct worlds with up to 99 other players.

This relates to the game's long-term ambition, which creative director Donald Mustard is becoming increasingly clear about.

Epic Games' Epic Game Plan

Fortnite's capacity to induce numerous seeming competitors to cooperate (or early "interoperability") with one another is the best indication of its potential. Fortnite is now available on every major entertainment platform – iOS, Android, PlayStation, Nintendo, PC, and Xbox – and allows complete cross-play across different identity/account systems, payment methods, social graphs, and generally locked ecosystems. The big gaming platforms fought for years, believing that allowing such an experience would undercut their network effects and lessen the need to acquire their proprietary gear. As a result, even though Sony and Microsoft knew they wanted to, a friend with Call of Duty on PlayStation could never play with a friend with Call of Duty on Xbox.

It's also uncommon for IP owners to allow their characters and stories to be mixed with other IPs. This happens occasionally (e.g., several Marvel v DC comic book crossovers and video games). But it's especially uncommon to see it in an experience they don't editorially control, let alone one based on unpredictability (not even the Fortnite creative team knows what it'll do in 2021) and with such a diverse spectrum of IP.

It is impossible to overstate the importance of organic evolution. These parties would never embrace interoperability or entrust their IP if you "announced" your aim to build a Metaverse. But, just as P&G can't say, "oh, Facebook isn't for us," most counterparties have no choice not to engage. They're probably keen to integrate into the "game" — Fortnite has become so popular and distinctive that most counterparties have no choice but to play. Fortnite is an extremely valuable platform.

It's a game called Fortnite. However, please re-ask that question in a year.

Epic is bringing far more to its Metaverse-building efforts than just a convincing on-ramp. Epic Games owns Unreal Engine 2, the second-largest independent game engine, in addition to running Fortnite, which was ostensibly a side project. Thousands of games (to simplify things) currently use its "stack" of tools and software, making it easy to exchange assets, integrate experiences, and share user profiles. Epic's game engine has become so sophisticated over time that it now supports a range of traditional media experiences. Unreal was used to shoot and render Disney's The Mandalorian, allowing director Jon Favreau to practically enter the digital sets to frame shots and arrange people. Audiences might freely explore most of these sets if Disney wishes – most of the settings and assets already exist. Unreal is increasingly used for live events outside of cinema and television, such as Fox Sports' NASCAR set.

Even Nevertheless, the Metaverse demands everyone, not only well-staffed organizations and technically talented individuals, to be able to generate and share 'content' and 'experiences.' Epic bought Twinmotion in April of last year for this purpose. The company was/is focused on providing straightforward, icon-based software that lets "architecture, construction, urban planning, and landscaping professionals" create realistic, immersive digital landscapes based on Unreal "in seconds," rather than VFX engineers or game designers. According to Epic Games CEO/Founder Tim Sweeney, this implies that there are now three ways to create in Unreal: the conventional "coding" engine itself, the more simple and "visual" Twinmotion, and Fortnite Creative Mode for users with no experience in programming and design. Each choice is likely to become more competent, user-friendly, and integrated over time. Epic's "Online Services" suite, which allows developers to support cross-play across Sony, Microsoft, Nintendo, PC, iOS, and Android while leveraging Epic's account systems and social graph, is becoming an increasingly essential aspect of the company's portfolio (which has 1.6B player connections). This isn't particularly unusual; Microsoft paid $400 million for PlayFab and spent millions more to support Xbox Live, while Amazon bought both GameSparks and GameLift to provide services to game creators that require a large number of servers and tools to run their online games. Valve doesn't provide server infrastructure, but its Steamworks solution provides free matchmaking and account services to developers — but exclusively for Valve's core business, the Steam Store. Epic's approach to Online Services is revealed in this way. Epic does not charge, unlike today's market leaders. It's also free to use with any engine, platform, or game. It also scales to the same size as Fortnite's player network, allowing any game to take advantage of the world's largest player graph to jumpstart their userbases. Although such a service has apparent value, Epic believes it is "more valuable if free" since it expands the company's already massive social graph, makes it much easier for additional games to "speak to" one another and allows players to bounce from experience to experience more smoothly. All of this calls into question Epic's dependence on Fortnite to construct the Metaverse. While Epic Online Services is still in private testing, the firm has stated that it would be available to the public in Q2 2020 and support "hundreds or thousands of games." It's also worth noting that all of this decreases Epic's reliance on Fortnite in its long-term Metaverse-building efforts.

Epic also runs one of the largest (if still tiny) digital game stores, allowing users to access various digital material and experiences. Few customers wanted more digital content fragmentation, and the majority were comfortable with market leader Steam. On the other hand, Epic Games Founder/CEO Tim Sweeney has been outspoken about how today's usual 30% commissions for digital content sales (e.g., iOS, Amazon, or Google Play) are not only usurious but also inhibit the formation of a truly digital world market. Consider what would happen if credit card fees were 60-20x higher than they are now; entire sections of the physical economy would be unable to function (such as a coffee shop or grocery store). Epic costs only 12% for this service (including the 5 percent Unreal licensing fee, too, making it only 7 percent for many customers). Notably, rumors continue that Sweeney sought even lower fees but ultimately agreed with his board at a rate of 12 percent - a figure he concedes does not always cover operating costs. This isn't to say there isn't a larger business here - running a storefront will undoubtedly contribute to the Metaverse's growth – but Sweeney's efforts appear to be far broader. He actively begs Google and Apple to match Epic's rates, despite the fact that they produce thousands of times the revenue of Epic's young store.

Here's how the 88 percent /12 percent retail battles would go if it were a coin toss: Heads, other stores aren't responding, therefore Epic Games Store triumphs, and all developers triumph. Tails, our competitors catch up to us, lose our revenue-sharing advantage, and other stores may gain, but all developers win.

Chapter 3:

WHO ELSE CAN BUILD THE METAVERSE?

Although the Metaverse has the potential to replace the Internet as a computing platform, it is unlikely to follow in the footsteps of its predecessor. The Internet was created by public research universities and government programs in the United States. This was partly because few in the private industry realized the commercial potential of the World Wide Web, but it was also because these organizations were effectively the only ones with the computational ability, resources, and goals to construct it. When it comes to the Metaverse, none of this is true.

Private industry isn't only fully aware of the Metaverse's potential; however, it also has the most assertive belief in its future, not to mention the most money (at least when it comes from a willingness to support Metaverse research and development), the best engineering skill, and the most conquest ambition. Companies want to control and define the Metaverse, not just be at the forefront of it. Although there are just a few possible leaders in the early Metaverse, open-source initiatives with a non-corporate mindset will continue to play an important role in the Metaverse and will attract some of the most interesting creative talents. And you will be able to identify each one.

Microsoft is an excellent example. With Office 365 and LinkedIn, the company has hundreds of millions of federated user identities, is the world's second-largest cloud vendor, has an extensive suite of work-related software and services that span all platforms/infrastructure/systems, clear technical experience in massive shared online content/operations, and a set of potential gateway experiences with Minecraft, Xbox + Xbox Live, and HoloLens. To this end, the Metaverse provides an opportunity for Microsoft to recapture the OS/hardware leadership it lost during the transition from PC to mobile. But, more crucially, CEO Satya Nadella recognizes that Microsoft must be present wherever work occurs. It is difficult to imagine Microsoft not being a significant driver in the virtualized future of labor and information processing, having successfully moved from enterprise to consumer, PC to mobile, and offline to online, all while keeping a prominent role in the "work" economy.

Despite the fact that Facebook CEO Mark Zuckerberg has not stated openly that he wants to establish and own the Metaverse, his preoccupation with it is evident. This is also clever. Facebook, more than any other corporation, stands to lose the most from the Metaverse, as it will create an even larger and more capable social graph, as well as a new computing and interaction platform. Simultaneously, the Metaverse enables Facebook to expand its reach up and down the stack. Despite multiple attempts to develop a smartphone operating system and launch consumer hardware, Facebook is the only FAAMG business solely focused on the app/service layer. Facebook might become the next Android or iOS/iPhone (thus Oculus), as well as a virtual goods version of Amazon, thanks to the Metaverse.

The Metaverse benefits of Facebook are enormous. It has more daily users, daily usage, and user-generated content than any other platform on the planet, as well as the second greatest percentage of digital ad, spend, billions in capital, thousands of world-class engineers, and a founder with majority voting rights. Its Metaverse assets are also fast developing, with patents for semiconductors and brain-to-machine computing interfaces currently among them. On the same hand, Facebook's track record as a platform for third-party developers/companies to build long-term enterprises, as a ringleader in a consortium (e.g., Libra), and managing user data/trust is bleak.

Amazon is intriguing in several ways. It will always strive to be the principal location where we purchase stuff.' It doesn't matter if it's purchased through a game engine, a virtual environment, or a web browser. Also, the company already has hundreds of millions of credit cards, the world's largest share of e-commerce (excluding China), is the world's largest cloud vendor, operates a variety of consumer media experiences (music, ebooks, video, video game broadcasting, audiobooks etc.) and third-party commerce platforms (e.g., Fulfilled by Amazon, Amazon Channels), and is developing what they hope will be the first major gaming/rendering engine purpose-built for the cloud.

More importantly, Jeff Bezos, the company's founder, and CEO is passionate about infrastructure investments. The web, for example, is powered by AWS (Amazon Web Services). Rather than buying and selling inventory directly, Amazon sells, packages, and distributes products sold by other firms, generating 80% of its revenue through "Fulfilled by Amazon" (like most retailers). While Elon Musk's private aerospace company, SpaceX, aspires to colonize Mars, Bezos has stated that his goal with Blue Origin is to "build gigantic chip factories in space and just send little bits down," similar to early web protocols and his AWS, so "we could build gigantic chip factories in space and simply send little bits down." As a result, Amazon is more likely than any other FAAMG business to support a completely "open" Metaverse – it doesn't need to control the UX or ID because it profits from massive growth in back-end infrastructure utilization and digital transactions.

The Internet is a data mine, and the Metaverse will contain both more data and potentially higher yields than the current web. And no one does a better job of monetizing this data on a worldwide scale than Google. Furthermore, the company is the market leader in indexing both the digital and physical worlds (almost 10,000 employees contribute to mapping activities), but it is also the most successful digital software and services company outside of China. It also runs the world's most popular operating system (Android) and the most open major consumer computing platform (Windows). Google was the first to go for the wearable computing opportunity with Google Glass aggressively and is now making a big push into digitizing the home with Google Assistant, its Nest suite of products, and FitBit, despite its failure. As a result, the Metaverse is likely to be the sole effort to bring together all of Google's disparate investments to date, including Stadia edge computing, Project Fi, Google Street View, massive dark fiber purchases, wearables, etc. virtual assistants, and more.

It's improbable that the underlying Metaverse will be driven or operated by it. True, it runs the world's second-biggest computing platform (and by far the most valuable), as well as the world's largest game retailers (which also means it pays more to developers than anyone else on earth). Furthermore, the corporation is aggressively investing in augmented reality gadgets and "connective tissue" to help the Metaverse (e.g., Apple Watch, Apple AirPods, beacons). However, Apple's mindset and commercial model are incompatible with creating an open platform for creation, where anybody can access the entire spectrum of user data and device APIs. That is to say, rather than the operator/driver, Apple is more likely to be the main method the Western world connects with Metaverse. This, like the Internet, will most likely work out well for everyone.

Unity will play a critical role if the Metaverse requires a broad interplay of assets, experiences, and shared APIs. More than half of mobile games use this engine, and it is even more frequently used in real-world rendering/simulation use cases (such as architecture, design, and engineering) than Unreal. While filmmaker Jon Favreau was producing and shooting the photo-realistic Lion King in Unity, he produced and shot Disney's The Mandalorian in Unreal. It also runs one of the largest digital ad networks in the world (a nice side effect of powering 10B daily minutes of mobile entertainment). However, it's unclear what role Unity will play in propelling the Metaverse forward. There is no store, no user account system, and no true direct-to-consumer experience. Most of its supplementary (non-engine or advertising) services aren't frequently used. Furthermore, most (though not all) Unity-powered games are simple mobile games rather than Metaverse gateways. However, given its unavoidable effect on standards, playtime, and content creation, it's difficult to picture it not being acquired and absorbed into a larger technology company with more assets and benefits.

Purchasing Unity used to be difficult to justify. Even though the company is extremely valuable, any potential buyer must keep Unity fully platform-agnostic to maintain market share, developer support, and influence (for example, Google couldn't make Unity exclusive to or best on Android/Chrome without alienating a large number of developers). This isn't to say that converting Unity into a proprietary engine isn't a good strategic move. The value lost as a result of such a decision and the premium required to purchase Unity will very certainly make such a move unaffordable. If, on the other hand, the purpose of a Unity acquisition is to secure a core role in the new Internet, the acquirer will have a motivation to maintain the engine open/available across platforms, and the price will quickly become immaterial.

Valve must have a plausible path to the Metaverse if Epic does. In terms of users, money, and playtime, Valve's Steam dwarfs the Epic Games Store. It is the owner of a number of the most popular and long-running multiplayer games (Counter-Strike, Team Fortress, DotA). In addition, the organization has a long history of monetization innovation and content (it was the first to experiment at scale with AAA free-to-play games and with player-to-player marketplaces). Likewise, Valve has spent years developing and launching virtual reality technology, earns billions in annual earnings, and is privately owned by a group of programmers who are passionate about open-source technologies and dislike closed environments. Simultaneously, Valve's Source engine has found minimal adoption, and unlike Epic, it does not appear to be focused on bringing its capabilities and assets together to build the Metaverse.

Why Does the Metaverse Involve Holograms?

When the internet was first introduced, it was followed by a series of technological breakthroughs, including the capacity to connect computers across large distances and the ability to link one web page to another. These technological characteristics provided the foundation for the abstract structures we now identify with the internet, such as webpages, applications, social networks, and everything else that relies on them. That's not even taking into account the convergence of non-internet interface innovations like displays, keyboards, mouse, and touchscreens, which are still necessary for the internet to function.

With the metaverse, there are some new building blocks in place, such as the capacity to host hundreds of people in an instance of a server (future versions of a metaverse should be able to handle thousands, if not millions) and motion-tracking tools that can distinguish where a person's hands are. These new technologies have the potential to be extremely intriguing and futuristic.

Several restrictions, however, may be impractical. When companies like Microsoft and Fa—Meta show fake movies of futuristic concepts, they gloss over how people interact with the metaverse. Virtual reality headsets are still clumsy, and most people experience motion sickness or physical pain after wearing them for long periods of time. Augmented reality glasses have similar issue, aside from the not-insignificant barrier of figuring out how to use augmented reality glasses in public without seeming like huge dorks.

So, how do IT companies show the concept of their technology without displaying the reality of massive equipment and strange glasses? So far, it appears that their main option is to develop technology from the ground up. Is it the holographic woman that appeared during Meta's talk? I'm sorry to break the news, but even with the most sophisticated versions of present technology, it's simply not possible.

Unlike motion-tracked digital avatars, which are a touch janky right now but might be better someday, regardless of what Iron Man says, there is no janky way of making a three-dimensional picture to appear in midair without carefully regulated circumstances. Perhaps they are supposed to be seen as pictures projected via glasses—after all, both women in the demo video are wearing glasses—but it assumes a lot about the physical capabilities of small glasses, which Snap can attest to being a difficult challenge to solve.

This type of deception of reality is widespread in in cinematic demonstration of how the metaverse may function. Is this individual using virtual reality gear or simply sitting at a desk? Is this person fastened to an immersive aerial rig or simply sitting at a desk? Another of Meta's demos showed individuals hovering in space—is this person strapped to an immersive aerial rig or just sitting at a desk? Does the person depicted by hologram wear a headset, and if so, how is their face scanned? A person may take virtual objects but hold them in what appear to be their actual hands at other times.

This demonstration raises many more questions than it responds to.

This is acceptable on certain levels. Microsoft, Meta, and any other company that does outlandish demos like these are trying to convey an aesthetic sense of what the future may be like, rather than addressing every technology issue. It's a long-standing tradition that extends back to AT&T's display of a voice-controlled folding phone that could magically erase people from photos and create 3D models, all of which seemed impossible at the time.

However, this kind of wishful-thinking-as-tech demonstration puts us in a position where it's difficult to anticipate which aspects of diverse metaverse ideas may one day become a reality. If virtual reality and augmented reality headsets become comfortable and economical enough for humans to wear on a daily—a huge "if"—then the notion of a virtual poker game in which your opponents are robots and holograms floating in space may become a reality. If not, you could always play Tabletop Simulator through a Discord video conference.

The gloss and glam of VR and AR also obscures the metaverse's more ordinary features, which are more likely to materialize. For example, it would be trivially easy for software firms to establish an open digital avatar standard, a form of file that contains attributes you would enter into a character creator—like eye color, hairstyle, or wardrobe options—and allows you to carry it about with you everywhere you go. There's no need to make more comfy VR headsets for that.

Aspects of the Metaverse: Opportunities, Risks and the Future

Metaverse has sparked a lot of debate in the past several years worldwide. People from many walks of life have responded enthusiastically to Metaverse's outreach.

"What's Next?" appeared on the British "Economist" website a few days ago. Metaverse, quantum computing, and virtual internet celebrities are among the 22 emerging technologies worth watching in 2022, according to the article "22 Emerging Technologies Worth Watching in 2022." According to the Commercial Press, metaverse was chosen as one of the "Top Ten Internet Terms in 2021" released by the National Language Resources Monitoring and Research Center on December 6.

According to the Commercial Press article, the term "metaverse" comes from the sci-fi notion of the novel "Avalanche" and currently refers to the virtual world created by advancements in technology such as XR (extended reality), digital twins, blockchain, and artificial intelligence (artificial intelligence). Internet apps and social life patterns that are integrated. The Metaverse is still a developing and evolving notion at this time. There are many debates around the world over the big and developing concept of the Metaverse.

How to treat the Metaverse?

Shen Xiangyang, a foreign academician of the United States National Academy of Engineering and a foreign academician of the Royal Academy of Engineering, recently discussed the new Metaverse meaning from the four levels of Metaverse in detail. He stated that the Metaverse should be a world that is defined by its openness and that subsequent products will build on it. We will collaboratively depict the outline of the Metaverse planet, which will be more intriguing, realistic, and warmer.

According to Tan Ping, the head of Alibaba Dharma Academy's XR laboratory, Metaverse is the future generation Internet, which is the full Internet on AR/VR glasses. AR/VR glasses are the next-generation mobile computing platform that will become mainstream, and Metaverse is the Internet industry's presentation on this new platform. In the Metaverse, every type of Internet application will have its presentation. Metaverse's technical foundations are organized into four layers: holographic construction, holographic simulation, virtual-reality fusion, and virtual-reality linkage. The first two layers use virtual reality (VR) to create a virtual environment, while the third and fourth layers use augmented reality (AR) to establish a hybrid of virtual and actual worlds.

The Metaverse, according to Zheng Weimin, an academician of the Chinese Academy of Engineering and a professor at Tsinghua University's Department of Computer Science and Technology, is a world made up of data, and distributed data storage has become the primary means of ensuring the Metaverse's long-term operation. Simultaneously, there is a hazy confluence of rights between data producers, managers, integrators, users, and other roles in the process of utilizing data, making it impossible to confirm the property rights of data pieces, leading to widespread data abuse. Blockchain is the foundational technology and architecture for resolving this set of issues. According to Academician Zheng

Weimin, computing power and data are the foundations for the growth of the Metaverse and the digital economy. Digital governance, financial technology, smart medical care, and smart manufacturing are examples of Internet innovation industries that demand processing capacity. Various industries have amassed a vast amount of data as my country's digital economy has grown, establishing a solid foundation for data lemmatization and marketization.

According to Nvidia CEO Jensen Huang, we want to recreate industries and plants in the Metaverse and the power infrastructure in the actual world. We can cut waste this way, which is one of the reasons why Metaverse will benefit businesses economically. They will be willing to spend billions of dollars to acquire artificial intelligence capabilities.

What's the chance?

TSMC Chairman Liu Deyin recently noted that the semiconductor industry's development has increased in tandem with global digitalization. AR might supplant smartphones in the next ten years, and VR could supplant computers. People will progressively encounter both the actual and virtual worlds. Metaverse's hardware requirements will continue to expand as it combines.

The founder and CEO of Ark Invest, Cathie Wood, believes Metaverse will be a trillion-dollar potential with far-reaching implications for the economy. This is a fantastic notion that, like technology, is likely to pervade every sector in ways we can't even comprehend right now.

According to Haim Israel, metaverse is a significant opportunity for blockchain technology, research managing director, and global strategist at Bank of America. Metaverse will also help mainstream cryptocurrency. The Metaverse is "the place where we will begin to use cryptocurrency as a form of payment." As a result, existing coins may experience excessive volatility. Certain types of stablecoins are predicted to dominate. Traditional payment businesses will be more interested in cryptocurrencies if cryptocurrencies are widely used in Metaverse, and there is expected to be a lot of interaction between the two.

According to reports, a special subject on digital economy was discussed at the 27th meeting of the Standing Committee of the 13th National People's

Congress of Jiangsu Province on December 6. According to Gao Qing, deputy head of the Jiangsu Development and Reform Commission, Metaverse might represent a new direction for future Internet development or a digital economy. The next stage of growth. It is necessary to integrate the application of network and computing power technology, display technology, Internet of things technology, artificial intelligence technology, blockchain technology, and many other cutting-edge digital technologies to support the Metaverse's open, anytime, anywhere, immersive, and other characteristics. Gao Qing also stated that to expand the digital economy, we must take risks and take advantage of new chances. We must aggressively promote Metaverse from idea to reality, accelerate the integration of digital technology to empower the real economy, and accelerate the digital transformation of our province's economy and society through the expansion of the Metaverse industry. It is vital to continue increasing support for metaverse development at several levels, including technology, standards, application, and law, and to lay a firm foundation for metaverse development.

Although Metaverse may take a long time to launch, Morgan Stanley believes that the following growth of NFTs and numerous social games would provide tremendous revenue prospects for the boutique industry. According to Morgan Stanley, around one-fifth of players on Roblox, a gaming platform that is presently considered a Metaverse pioneer, change their game avatars every day. By 2030, social games are estimated to generate $20 billion in revenue for the digital luxury goods market. Various digital luxury items and collectibles may obtain a stake of more than US$25 billion in the US$300 billion NFT market. Morgan Stanley claims that the company's numerous forays into the realm of NFT and social gaming have aided in developing new consumer groups and a better understanding of this emerging market. For NFT and Metaverse games, the brand is in the idea verification stage. The evidence reveals that the present tests are all successful; the next step is to figure out how to make it happen.

Microsoft CEO Satya Nadella expressed his interest in Metaverse on November 19th, saying that he will continue to apply full-stack thinking to embrace new development opportunities like Metaverse. The Metaverse, according to Nadella, connects the physical and digital worlds, bringing people, things, and fields together in the commercial and consumer Internet. Because integration may be conceivable, it should not be seen as a distinct consumer market or an enterprise-level market phenomenon. It is required. In some ways, the epidemic's popularity of video conferencing has given us some experience with a 2D Metaverse. Beyond time and space, the 3D Metaverse is unquestionably a significant growth direction.

What risks should be vigilant?

Shen Yang, Executive Director of the New Media Research Center of Tsinghua University's School of Journalism, presented the team's "Metaverse Development Research Report 2020-2021" at the "China Development Forum Young Entrepreneurs Summit" on December 6th. Metaverse, according to Shenyang, is the most advanced kind of mobile Internet currently available. However, because the Metaverse sector is still in its infancy, it exhibits the immaturity and instability associated with developing industries, and there are numerous potential concerns. The Metaverse industry as a whole is currently in a "sub-healthy" state, with at least ten key risk factors. The industry and the market must return to sanity as soon as possible. Capital manipulation, public opinion bubbles, ethical restrictions, monopolistic tensions, industry involution, computing power pressure, economic risks, addiction risks, privacy concerns, and challenges with intellectual property protection are among the 10 primary hazards.

360's founder, Zhou Hongyi, spoke about Metaverse. He stated that this concept is really popular. Because of the high stock price, many people have finally found a new way to make money. Metaverse, in my opinion, is a virtual reality of fiction. It has created an entirely online universe separate from the offline world. It will take some time. Second, I observe Facebook's thoughts and follow their futuristic fantasies. I believe This does not depict humanity's future. I believe it indicates humanity's demise. It suggests that everyone will live in an imaginary space if we get rid of reality and do not go through such rigorous efforts to reach a goal in reality. I've spoken with some colleagues in the United States. They believe that the

Metaverse's highest destiny is the integration of brain-computer interfaces. You can generate limitless numbers by activating your brain waves as long as you close your eyes and lie down in bed with a tube for nutritional solution inserted. In the movie "The Matrix," will illusion and image finally replace the human battery? Human society will not progress as a result of the Metaverse. To overcome the energy crisis, humanity must tackle the challenge of nuclear fusion. Only until mankind has solved the riddle of cosmic navigation will he be able to leave the planet.

Multiple companies claim to be doing Metaverse, but they are many Internet products, many of which are merely mobile products, not "Metaverse," according to Professor Shen Yang of Tsinghua University's School of Journalism and Communication's New Media Research Center. "Now that the metaverse is already boiling, I'd like to add to it." I hope that people of the era can use and satisfy steadily improving technology, from processing power to communication technology, algorithms, and final products. The phrase "metaverse" is the newest buzzword in the IT industry, especially since Facebook changed its name to Meta last month to reflect its business transformation. To be clear, no one has heard of Metaverse. Because the concept is still in its early phases, no one knows what it will look like. Its development, however, must be demand-driven. Metaverse has been enlisted by IT heavyweights such as Meta, Microsoft, and Nvidia to investigate the application of various technologies in various settings. But, whatever the case, The ideals on which these products are built must, in the end, fulfill the demands of people. Products that do not match customers' needs will almost certainly be phased out of the market.

On November 15, Russian President Vladimir Putin said at the 2021 "AI Journey" International Conference (AI Journey 2021), according to press reports: "I'd like to point out that the term metaverse was coined 30 years ago by a well-known figure. According to the science fiction writer's vision, people have escaped from the imperfect actual world to the metaverse. For us now, such a notion is far too dismal. I don't think there's any reason to follow this route." Putin "We need to leverage the metaverse's function so that individuals may communicate, work, learn, and conduct joint innovation and commercial initiatives together no matter how far apart," he continued. Putin believes that this is critical for technology companies, creative industries, virtual reality and mixed reality equipment manufacturers, and even legal scholars who must formulate the economic and social norms of this "new world." "This is a difficulty," he said. This includes safeguarding the safety of persons in cyberspace and the safety of their virtual avatars in the "Metaverse," according to Putin. With the help of virtual worlds, technology developers claim that individuals would travel through space without ever leaving their homes. "This allows individuals to communicate with others on different continents," Putin remarked.

How long has it been on the ground?

Hon Hai Chairman Guo Taiming recently visited the press conference of the iCareDx medical technology exhibition, a startup firm founded with personal investment, and voiced his thoughts on the concept of "Metaverse" at the event, according to news published on December 5th. According to Terry Gou, the Metaverse concept will take 5 to 10 years to implement, and associated applications are still a long way off. Although there are several R&D opportunities in the development process, the emphasis is overly placed on the application side. The "user experience" still has a lot of space for improvement, so talking about application explosion isn't feasible right now.

Disney CEO Bob Chapek and Kraft CEO Robert Kraft conducted a meeting in Boston on November 16th. The two sides addressed Metaverse, with Chapek implying that Metaverse will be Disney's future. He claimed that Disneyland and the Disney+ internet platform gave the corporation unequaled Metaverse building capabilities. He claims that this three-dimensional canvas will bring the physical and digital worlds together seamlessly and unrestrictedly, allowing for more creative thinking. He feels that Metaverse is the next generation's development path. He also predicted the future, predicting that in the Metaverse, fans will eat lunch with Disney princesses.

According to Zuo Pengfei, deputy director of the Institute of Quantitative and Technological Economics of the Chinese Academy of Social Sciences' Informatization and Network Economics Research Office and secretary-general of the Chinese Academy of Social Sciences' Informatization Research Center, we are about 10-20 years away from realizing the Metaverse's basic scenario. The Metaverse will have a huge impact on five aspects of our lives and social and economic development: the first is to improve social production efficiency through technological innovation and collaboration methods; the second is to birth a slew of new technologies, formats, and models, as well as to promote traditions. The third is to promote cross-border derivation of the cultural and creative industries, which greatly stimulates information consumption; the fourth is to reconstruct working life styles, as much work and life will take place in the virtual world; and the fifth is to promote the construction of smart cities and innovative social governance models.

Chapter 4:

WHAT'S THE METAVERSE LIKE RIGHT NOW?

The paradox of defining the metaverse is that it necessitates the definition of the present in order to describe the future. MMOs, which are basically virtual worlds, digital concerts, online avatars, video calls with people all over the world, commerce platforms, are already available. So, there has to be something novel about them to market these objects as a new way of looking at the world.

If you talk about the metaverse long enough, someone will likely bring up fictional works like Snow Crash, which coined the term "metaverse," or Ready Player One, which portrays a virtual reality world where everyone works, shops, and plays. When mixed with the broader pop-culture concept of holograms and heads-up displays (basically everything Iron Man has utilized in his previous ten movies), these stories serve as a creative reference point for the metaverse—a metaverse in which tech corporations may offer us something new.

That type of panic is as much a part of the metaverse as any other. It's no wonder, however, that proponents of NFTs—cryptographic tokens that, in a sense, operate as certificates of ownership for digital items—are enthusiastic about the metaverse notion. Sure, NFTs are bad for the environment, but if these tokens can be considered the digital key to your Roblox virtual mansion, then they're worth it. You've just transformed your meme-collecting pastime into a vital component of the internet's infrastructure (and maybe increased the value of all that cryptocurrency you own.)

It's important to remember all of this because, while it's easy to compare today's proto-metaverse concepts to the early internet and assume that everything would develop and expand in a linear fashion, this isn't always the case. It's not certan people will want to sit in a virtual workplace without their legs or play poker with Dreamworks CEO Mark Zuckerberg, much alone that AR and VR technology will ever become as common as smartphones and PCs.

It's possible that any true "metaverse" consist primarily of interesting VR games and digital avatars in Zoom calls but predominantly of what we presently refer to as the internet.

Making Money In The Metaverse

New technologies are exploding out of control, and enormous sums of money are being exchanged. Artists and small businesses are being hailed as forerunners of a new era.

You'd be forgiven if you didn't know everything. The phenomenon I'm describing takes place in a parallel universe.

The "metaverse" is a merging of our physical and digital lives brought on by advances in internet connectivity, augmented reality/virtual reality, and blockchain. It's the conclusion of all of our science fiction fantasies—what 'Tron' and 'Ready Player One' envisioned, but which is already happening.

If that sounds intriguing to you, it's no surprise that people are making significant investments in the space. The metaverse's chosen money, the non-fungible token, has received almost $400 million in funding (or NFT). That 40 million dollars change hands per month, and that the most costly NFT transactions in history have all occurred in the last few months. Last week, Christie auctioned off a piece of Beeple's digital art for more than $69 million via NFT.

Many people don't understand Upland by any traditional metric. It's more than a virtual game; it's a communal experience, but why are tens of thousands of people spending their hard-earned money on it? One reason could be that it's so unusual.

Upland is a decentralized application (dApp) that allows users to purchase, sell, and trade virtual real estate using real-world maps. You may go to Upland in New York City to see who owns the Empire State Building or the New York Stock Exchange, for example. If you have enough in-game currency, you can even bid for them yourself.

This concept is intriguing on its own. But it's the way Upland's in-game economy operates that makes it more than just a toy. Players begin by purchasing UPX, the native token, using fiat money to purchase their first properties. Over time, as Upland grows more popular, market prices for these properties will naturally rise. Virtual landlords have the option of holding or cashing out for fiat.

Although Upland homes are virtual, they are extremely real investment assets. Consider the New York Stock Exchange. In comparison to other Upland properties, you'd think the Stock Exchange could bring a decent amount of UPX. But do you think it's worth the entire $23,000? That's how much it sold for in December of last year. It is now even more valuable.

Even still, the financial aspect of Upland's attractiveness does not entirely convey it. We spoke with Dirk Lueth, one of the platform's co-founders, to get the full picture of this story. We asked him how much money players can make on his platform and what they like about it. He narrowed it down to five factors:

• Excited about the perspective of rebuilding the world and eventually making a living in it

• Fun to find properties that have a special value, meaning or emotional attachment

• Finding like-minded people

• Enjoying the community, making friends

• Thrill to flip properties

• Excited about the perspective of rebuilding the world and eventually making a living in it

Upland's development team wants to expand its environment in the coming months and years by adding 3D property construction features and allowing users to manage businesses in-game. They're also working on a feature that will allow players to incorporate NFT artwork into their virtual properties, boosting their value the same way that physical art does for real estate.

"I'm extremely thrilled to bring more real-world brands into Upland, and finally to introduce some location-based services and features to begin blurring the actual world with the Upland metaverse," Lueth said.

Why Are Established Brands Getting Involved?

The metaverse is still mostly unknown, with only the most forward-thinking technologists taking note. How much longer will it be like this? According to Lueth, more traditional game publishers are dabbling in blockchain. It will be extremely difficult for them to avoid disrupting their business model.

Because businesses recognize the marketing and direct money potential, we'll see more NFTs for everything (plenty of consumer goods will get NFTied and appear in metaverses). As more industries enter the space, some may experiment with new types of products and business models using their brands.

Lueth's enthusiasm for the metaverse's future is palpable, but he is cautious about projecting how long it will take for popular adoption. In both cases, he's probably correct. The ceiling is high, and the timetable is lengthy.

Nonetheless, a few well-known figures have begun to dangle their toes in the metaverse. Take, for example, Sotheby's, which recently sold an NFT painting for a staggering price.

There's also Atari, which is synonymous with the early days of gaming. The business has recently leapfrogged the entire current generation of gaming by establishing its cryptocurrency, Atari Token, in a move few could have predicted. I chatted with Fred Chesnais, the company's CEO, who had a daring idea for the project.

"With the Atari Token, we're laying a foundation for other legacy gamers to build on." We're going where previous legacy gaming firms haven't gone before. "We're pursuing the most cutting-edge blockchain technology that will genuinely connect blockchain with gaming for a next-generation virtual experience," Chenais added.

Atari Token's mission is to become the cryptocurrency token of choice in the video game and entertainment sectors. It will help developers and gamers successfully monetize their digital assets by providing a market for rapid and straightforward token transfers, backed by the promises of smart contract technology.

Atari's recent cooperation with Enjin, possibly the largest cryptocurrency firm in the blockchain gaming space, is one example of how it works. The two firms have collaborated to develop an NFT fashion line where users can use their cryptocurrency to purchase Atari-branded clothes.

Atari intends to expand its presence into other markets in the future, such as Africa, where mobile game creation is booming. They're also in the process of developing immersive and powerful virtual and augmented reality games. Chesnais is very enthusiastic about it.

"It's a desire to build (as many as feasible) various digital worlds in addition to the real world. People are more aware than ever of the genuine value that virtual worlds provide. People have been lured to digital interactive experiences ever since Atari launched the business with PONG," said the Atari CEO. "This, together with NFTs, which allow users to own their in-game assets while really empowering artists, is driving more interest. And this upward tendency will continue. We're still in the early stages."

Visual Business Models Aren't the Only Thing

Jason Fox, CEO of EarBuds, was another CEO we spoke with on the new metaverse business models succeeding. After being on the field and wondering what

Cam Newton was listening to inside his headphones, Fox, a former NFL player, came up with the idea for the startup. That's how the concept of creating a social music app occurred to him. While his company isn't on the visual side of the metaverse, audio and voice are becoming increasingly significant.

"As Clubhouse and other social speech apps have grown in popularity, audio is becoming an increasingly important aspect of how we connect electronically. But this is about more than just voice - music is an important aspect of our identity in the real world, and we know it's also important for how people express themselves online. Listening to and finding new music has always been a group activity, but streaming has transformed it into a more personal one, typically guided by an algorithm. "With EarBuds, we're reintroducing music as a social experience."

Chapter 5:

FUTURE OF THE METAVERSE ECONOMY

The CEO of IMVU sees the metaverse coming.

The team behind IMVU provided some of the most insightful thoughts on metaverse economics among the pioneers we spoke with.

With seven million monthly active users, IMVU is considered one of the world's largest 3D avatar social platforms. They have a marketplace with over 50 million items, a native cryptocurrency (VCOIN) that has already generated millions of dollars in income and has recently raised $35 million in funding. All of this puts it in the top tier of metaverse businesses, gaming or not.

Daren Tsui, their CEO, quickly pointed out the larger context and climate that allowed IMVU to grow when we chatted with him.

The term "metaverse" first appeared in Neal Stephenson's 1992 book Snow Crash, but the concept of a virtual simulation where people can interact with one another had already existed (for example, Tron in 1982). "As related technology advances over time, the realism and capabilities of virtual experiences have dramatically improved, drawing more users to connect in the virtual world," said Tsui.

There is little doubt, according to Tsui, that the pandemic has prompted many more people throughout the world to look for a safer and more effective method to socialize online. They've discovered a fun and exciting way to connect and communicate with new acquaintances in real life.

COVID-19-induced social separation makes sense as a driver of interest in virtual social platforms. Tsui, on the other hand, is focused on the long term. The epidemic, in his opinion, is driving more people to "seek for" something like the metaverse, but the "dramatically" better "realism and capacities of virtual experiences" is the reason they're staying—coming back, spending money. When the pandemic is done, that won't go away.

We can see what he's talking about, thanks to Upland, Atari, EarBuds, and IMVU. Upland is already offering an unrivaled investment-platform-slash-gaming experience that will be nearly unrecognizable in just a few years if all of the things they're experimenting with are implemented. Atari's vintage gaming knowledge is being used in a new, cutting-edge approach to in-game item trade. IMVU has created a virtual environment that people want to be a part of. They may be attracted to the pandemic, but they're also attending virtual events and purchasing avatar items because it's entertaining and immersive.

Tsui put it quite succinctly. When asked when our physical world and the metaverse will collide to create something even bigger, better, and more memorable than what exists today, he simply stated, "It's not if, but when."

UNDERSTANDING THE METAVERSE THROUGH REAL-WORLD EXAMPLES

The phrase "metaverse" has been bandied about in recent months, particularly when Facebook announced its rebranding as Meta. Meta is a social technology startup with the mission of "bringing the metaverse to life." Many people in the metaverse were intrigued by this.

The name and concept aren't new in and of themselves. In truth, concepts and examples of the metaverse have been around for several decades. In Neal Stephenson's 1992 novel Snow Crash, the characters utilize computer avatars to explore a digital world or engage with each other to escape their dystopian reality; the term "metaverse" was coined.

David Gelernter first proposed the concept of a digital twin, or a virtual duplicate of something that exists in real life, in his book Mirror Worlds in 1991. Dr. Michael Grieves, credited as the inventor of the digital twin software concept, first applied the digital twin concept to manufacturing in 2002. In 2010, NASA employed digital twin technology to simulate space capsules.

The metaverse appears to be upon us, but what is it, and what impact could it have on our daily lives?

Here are few examples that help you understand the metaverse, how it works, and where it might be headed in the future.

Understanding the Metaverse through Real-World Examples:

It's difficult to narrow down a precise definition of the metaverse.

The metaverse is a loosely defined virtual universe where users have access to digital avatars that allow them to "live" in this virtual reality. People can communicate with friends, acquire and sell digital assets, go to virtual locales (which may be entirely imagined or have real-life parallels), and more in the metaverse.

The metaverse promises a world of limitless possibilities, similar to the OASIS in Ready Player One, where the user's imagination is the only limit.

To put it another way, the metaverse is a virtual universe that exists in addition to or as an extension of our physical world. It's made up of interoperable technologies like virtual reality and augmented reality, and it works on a functional digital economy powered by digital currencies or cryptocurrencies—and no, digital currencies and cryptocurrencies are not the same things.

Furthermore, there is no single, distinct metaverse. There are a lot of iterations in the metaverse. For example, if you're playing Fortnite, you can enter a metaverse. If you use Facebook Horizon, you can also access a distinct metaverse. On the other hand, the metaverse is designed to be interoperable, which means you'll eventually be able to access assets acquired on one platform and use them on another.

Metaverse Examples that Help Explain the Metaverse

The metaverse's concept and the possibilities it opens up are just incredible. Here are some real-world instances of the metaverse and where it will help better describe this parallel reality.

THE METAVERSE IN POP CULTURE

- Ready Player One

Ready Player One is almost frequently used as an example when discussing the metaverse. There is, however, a valid reason for this. Ernest Cline's science fiction novel from 2011 presents a vivid image of what the metaverse might look like and how it might function.

In the novel, set in 2045, people turn to the OASIS, a massively multiplayer online simulation game (MMOSG) with its virtual world (and currency) where they can interact with other players, visit different locations, play games, and even shop, to escape a world ravaged by war, poverty, and climate change. The OASIS is a world where anything can happen—people's imaginations only constrain "reality," and anyone can be whatever they wish.

If all of that is too much for you, watch the 2018 Steven Spielberg film adaptation, which gives a decent look at the book's metaverse.

Facebook is well on its way to launching Facebook Horizon, its own version of the OASIS in the real world. The Oculus Rift or the Oculus Quest 2 headgear must enter this virtual world. Users can explore, play, create, and engage with other players in this vast digital environment.

- Fortnite Concerts

What began as a game has swiftly evolved into something more complex and capable of providing a wider range of experiences.

Players in Fortnite can create their worlds and embark on adventures. They can play with other Fortnite gamers in the community. The game's crossplay feature allows players to play it on various platforms, including Xbox, PC, Playstation, and mobile phones.

Fortnite has evolved into more than just a game, with players able to hang out and attend in-game concerts. Travis Scott, Ariana Grande, and Marshmello were among the performers who performed. Fortnite's developer, Epic Games, raises the stakes by launching the Soundwave Series, which includes music from musicians all around the world. The Series gives gamers access to in-game interactive experiences.

Games and Social Networks in the Metaverse

- Second Life

Second Life is an online environment where users may create digital avatars and explore the world, connect with other users, and sell products and services using the Linden Dollar, the in-world money.

Second Life is a forerunner of the metaverse, in which users can interact with one another and the digital world in a shared virtual realm. It has been around since the late 2000s and allows users to explore the metaverse's potential.

- The Sandbox

The Sandbox is a virtual metaverse where people can create and play in virtual environments. It also allows them to control and profit from their in-game experiences. Non-fungible tokens, or NFTs, can be used to buy and trade lands and assets in The Sandbox metaverse.

NFTs are virtual tokens that are generated on the blockchain. This makes them one-of-a-kind, indivisible, and non-transferable, allowing you to own your in-game assets digitally.

This demonstrates the metaverse's rising acceptance of digital money. In a digital future, we will be able to perceive, use, and define money in ways that are currently unimaginable.

- Illuvium

Illuvium is a 2022 release that is described as an open-world roleplaying game based on the Ethereum Blockchain. Illuvials are deity-like beings that may be stored on Shards, and players hunt and catch them here. Players in Illuvium essentially collect NFTs, which symbolize each Illuvial. You'll also be able to accumulate in-game products that you may sell on third-party NFT marketplaces.

Chapter 6:

AUGMENTED REALITY (AR)

Augmented reality is a technology that combines real-world aspects with digital enhancements. For example, you may be in the real world yet see a dragon perched on your neighbor's car if you use augmented reality.

It's already used in a lot of games and navigation systems. Pokémon Go is one of the most popular AR applications, allowing players to hunt for, fight against, and capture Pokémon that "appear" in the real world using their phone's camera.

AR is also employed in navigation systems, in addition to gaming applications. Google's AR and VR technologies allow users to explore the actual world more.

This real-world software aims to provide users with a more immersive experience, allowing them to get the most out of their smart devices. For example, when you use Google Maps' Live View, you can traverse an area more easily because directions are superimposed on top of your Google Street View photographs.

Another application is the ability to employ augmented reality in Google Search. This allows you to set 3D things in your area and better understand their scale.

Other real-world applications of AR include:

• illustrating plays in football games

• giving you an idea of what a piece of furniture may look like in your room

• bringing historical places to life by overlaying pictures of old civilizations over ruins

AR technology is also finding its way into the classroom. The Metaverse Studio is an augmented reality platform that allows teachers and students to develop augmented reality in their classrooms. It may be used to construct apps, games, and activities to supplement project-based learning.

The Evolution of Augmented Reality

In 2016, the Pokemon Go craze propelled augmented reality (AR) mainstream. Although it appeared to be cutting-edge technology when people worldwide were 'catchin' 'em all,' AR was invented in 1968.

Did you know that the first instance of augmented reality was in 1968?

From the first computer-generated visuals and projections in the 1960s and 1970s to the most recent AR games and Microsoft HoloLens Developer Kit, the usage and potential of augmented reality are constantly evolving. In 2016, the total investment in augmented and virtual reality was €925 million, with no signs of slowing.

AR then and now

Ivan Sutherland built the first head-mounted display system in 1968, which was AR's start. The Air Force used AR to create virtual fixtures, and NASA used it to improve visual navigation testing. Tom Caudell, a Boeing researcher, created the phrase "augmented reality" in 1990. AR and the internet eventually came together in the early 2000s, but interest in the technology didn't take off until 2009, thanks to the smartphone revolution. Because of the growth in smart wear technologies, augmented reality has recently undergone a second renaissance.

Augmented Reality (AR) in business

Apart from the 'conventional' usage of AR technology in gaming, various new possibilities and benefits have emerged in other industries such as logistics, manufacturing, retail, and many more. AR can benefit any process or business activity that can benefit from a visual overlay.

Businesses are embracing AR's potential. Boeing, for example, conducted an experiment in which a group of factory trainees assembled an airplane wing using AR instructions. The results revealed a 30 percent time reduction and a 90% increase in inaccuracy. Similarly, DHL is testing AR-enabled smartglasses in one of its warehouses to enhance efficiency by 25% and is currently looking into a wider rollout.

Retail is another industry that uses AR technology to improve the customer experience. Ikea has launched virtual furniture, allowing buyers to see Ikea products in their kitchens and living rooms before purchasing. Lego is working on a Digital Box that allows youngsters to grasp a virtual replica of their toy and turn and shape it with their hands to discover it from all sides.

Metaverse Real Estate

We can't talk about the metaverse without including real estate applications. People purchase and sell properties on digital marketplaces just like they do in the real world. They are, however, trading in cryptocurrencies.

While metaverse real estate is still regarded as "extremely speculative," engineers predict the metaverse will eventually develop its own fully functioning economy. The popularity of virtual real estate has led to the sale of digital assets for millions of dollars. A plot of virtual land in Decentraland was sold for 618,000 mana ($2.4 million in crypto), while a parcel of virtual land in The Sandbox was sold for $4.3 million.

Because of the metaverse's growing popularity, many businesses have decided to create their digital worlds and, with them, digital properties. The Metaverse Group, for example, runs Decentraland, a virtual environment that its users entirely control. Users can explore lands owned by other users, create artwork and challenges, engage in events to earn rewards, and exchange digital assets using mana, Decentraland's sort of coinage, just like in other virtual worlds.

SuperWorld, a virtual environment where you may buy, sell, and accumulate pieces of virtual land, is another outstanding example of real estate in the metaverse. Mount Rushmore (0.1 ETH), the Taj Mahal (50 EHT), and the Eiffel Tower are among the 64.8 billion distinct parcels of virtual property it has to date (selling for 100 ETH).

Users who buy a piece of virtual real estate become owners of unique digital assets and platform stakeholders who can share money generated by user activities on the land.

What the Metaverse Could Spell Out for Our Future

The metaverse is gradually taking shape. It has found its way into various areas of our lives, from games and movies to real-world navigation systems. While the metaverse is difficult to define and is still in its early stages of development, we can say for now that it is brimming with potential. What remains to be seen is what else the metaverse has in store for us in the future.

Virtual Reality in Metaverse

Since its introduction to the public, virtual reality has mostly been promoted as a novel and exciting way to play video games. The most popular headgear, such as Facebook's Oculus, HTC's Vive, and Sony's PlayStation VR, boast their capacity to elevate the game experience.

In recent years, there has been a shift toward identifying new and alternative use-cases for virtual reality. Virtual reality is currently being used and tested in various fields, including education, sports, mental and physical health, shopping, and more. The metaverse is a much larger, more aggressive objective for virtual reality recently discussed. Indeed, Facebook has announced ambitions to hire 10,000 people in the European Union over the next five years to assist in creating a metaverse. So, what is the metaverse, and how will virtual reality be incorporated into it?

Defining the Metaverse

It can be difficult to explain the metaverse, which some people refer to as Web3. This is primarily because one does not yet exist. People have, however, provided their metaverse views, which we shall use as a guide. Consider the metaverse to be an immersive, 3D, and communal virtual reality. Users would be brought into the virtual environment in the same way they would be in a virtual reality video game if they wore a VR headset.

Accessibility

How will users access the metaverse now that we have a fundamental grasp of it? VR headsets are currently the most widely accepted technique of accessing the virtual universe. VR headsets may not be required to enter the metaverse in the future, but for the time being, they are the most promising option. This helps explain why firms like Facebook spend extensively on virtual reality headsets and virtual reality in general. Listen to our audio episode with special guest Luke Levene, VP of Sales at XRApplied, for additional information on the present state of virtual reality technology, where it is headed, and current VR trends.

Exploring the Metaverse

You might wonder what makes the metaverse so special since we already have virtual reality. Virtual reality and the metaverse have significant distinctions. First and foremost, consider virtual reality as the ship and the metaverse as the destination. Furthermore, users can do much more than play games in the metaverse, which is currently the most popular use case for virtual reality. Users will be able to socialize with other humans worldwide, shop, conduct business, and more in the metaverse.

Furthermore, cryptocurrency will play an important role. Visionaries have expressed a desire for metaverses to have their coins and the ability to pay with other cryptocurrencies. NFTs, unsurprisingly, will play an important role in the metaverse.

The Role of NFTs

The inclusion of NFTs is one of the metaverse's most important features. Whether it's an image, soundtrack, meme, virtual clothing piece, magazine article, or other kind of digital art, NFTs are commonly viewed as such. However, in terms of the metaverse, NFTs have a completely different application. In the metaverse, NFTs can represent land.

There should be a finite amount of land created in each metaverse. This results in scarcity. According to the rule of supply and demand, scarcity raises value. As in the actual world, users in the metaverse will acquire land in the form of an NFT, just as they would in the real world. They can then keep the NFT for as long as they like and sell it (along with the land) when they're ready.

In reality, land is already being sold in virtual worlds as NFTs. Republic Realm, a digital real estate investment firm, purchased land in Decentraland in the form of an NFT for $913,000. Decentraland is a virtual reality platform built on Ethereum. Minecraft players can now use Minecraft currency to buy land in the game. The land that was purchased was also in the form of an NFT.

Key Players

The traditional tech heavyweights such as Facebook, Microsoft, Amazon, and Snap are the primary players in the battle to construct a metaverse. Additionally, huge firms such as Nvidia and Roblox, who are not household brands but are significantly investing in the metaverse, are not yet household names.

Nvidia is a company that makes computer graphics processors, automotive chipsets, and robotics chipsets and invests extensively in artificial intelligence. On the other hand, Roblox is an online gaming platform that allows players to share games that they have developed and created. Both firms are important participants in the game industry. Thus their involvement in the metaverse movement is not surprising.

The metaverse is a vast endeavor that customers may not be able to participate in for decades, if at all. Virtual reality is a significant part of the process as corporations struggle to turn their dreams for these artificial worlds into reality. Who knows, maybe new technologies will arise when the metaverse is ready for consumer adoption, and virtual reality will be obsolete.

How Augmented Reality Works In Metaverse

People were transported to a kaleidoscopic world of flying fish and friendly robots when Facebook displayed a mock-up of the "metaverse" — apparently the internet of the future.

While even Facebook CEO Mark Zuckerberg admits that such experiences may be years away, other proponents say that a more limited form of the metaverse is now available.

"In some ways, we're in the early beginnings of the metaverse," Peggy Johnson, CEO of Magic Leap, said on Tuesday at the Web Summit in Lisbon.

Magic Leap produces augmented reality (AR) headsets that have already been used by surgeons preparing to separate conjoined twins and factory supervisors conducting site inspections.

In both situations, information regarding what the users saw appeared in front of their eyes.

It may not be as intense — or as bizarre — as the virtual reality (VR) experiences that Zuckerberg hopes to bring to people's homes in the future. However, it blurs the physical and digital worlds, which is a major concept in the metaverse.

"With virtual reality, you put on a device, and you're transported to another world," Johnson explained. "With augmented reality, you put on a gadget, and you're still in your world, but we're adding digital stuff to it."

In this screen picture from a video broadcast Oct. 28, an avatar of Facebook CEO Mark Zuckerberg is seen carrying a US flag while riding a hydrofoil in the "Metaverse" during a augmented reality and live-streamed virtual conference to announce the rebranding of Facebook as Meta. | VIA REUTERS/FACEBOOK

Many people's experiences with augmented reality have so far been restricted to playing Pokemon Go or experimenting with image filters that place a set of amusing ears on someone's face.

However, the genuine promise of AR is beginning to be realized in health care, according to Johnson.

"You can bring in specialists from all over the world to look at the same thing you are," she explained. "You can draw digital lines where you think the incision will be made after surgery."

Magic Leap's initial ambition to bring augmented reality to the masses created a lot of buzzes and approximately $2.3 billion in venture capital funding when it was founded in 2010.

It was originally envisioned that it would transport a killer whale into a gymnasium full of youngsters.

However, when Magic Leap's first headset was ultimately unveiled in 2018, it was met with significant dissatisfaction; the equipment was too cumbersome and pricey for the general public to adopt.

Last year, the company was forced to lay off roughly half of its workforce.

In August 2020, Johnson, a former Microsoft executive, took over as CEO and shifted the company's focus to developing professional eyewear.

Last month, the Florida-based business announced an additional $500 million in funding, with a new headset, the Magic Leap 2, expected to be released in 2022.

The new version is lighter, but it's still designed for people who are used to wearing goggles at work, such as surgeons doing sensitive work or defense sector professionals.

Google Glass, a pair of "smart glasses" that failed to catch on when they debuted in 2014, has resurfaced as a professional-oriented offering.

Johnson believes it will be "a few more years" until Magic Leap or one of its competitors develops an AR headset that can be worn by people all around the world.

However, Johnson believes that this is the point at which AR will truly revolutionize our lives.

She proposed that it might allow us to see restaurant reviews pinging in front of our eyes as we walk down a street, looking at the possibilities.

Have you forgotten who someone's name is? It's no problem. It may appear above their head as they approach you.

"Right now, we're all staring at our phones," Johnson explained. She hopes that augmented reality will better absorb the world around us — a world with additional information put on top of it.

If the revolution occurs, the market may become overcrowded. Facebook is reportedly developing its augmented reality headgear, and Apple is following suit. Snapchat's developer, Snap, is meanwhile trialing a new pair of its "Spectacles" on AR artists.

Chapter 7:

THE INVESTMENT OF NTF'S IN THE METAVERSE

Why NFTs Are The Vital To Accessing The Metaverse
- Metaverses provide a fair and open economy aided by the blockchain
- The play-to-earn gaming economy will empower players of blockchain games through NFTs
- NFTs are the bridge to the metaverse and facilitate identity, social experiences in the metaverse
- Users can collect in-game tokens to get started

NFTs are ushering in a new era of the digital world - the Metaverse - with their rapidly expanding use cases. Facebook's launch of Meta, signaling the shift towards a metaverse era, where NFT-based augmented experiences are likely to act as pillars for next-generation social networks, best exemplifies the coming of metaverses on the world scene.

NFTs and metaverses are already intertwined, particularly in blockchain gaming and other interoperable games, where they serve as value carriers for large-scale digital social media. NFT gaming is popular, despite being a relatively new concept, as evidenced by Binance NFT's Initial Game Offering (IGO). This new gaming arm has garnered such positive feedback from gamers and crypto consumers that it has already surpassed $16 million in trade volume in just two weeks, with all IGO's NFT collections sold out.

A metaverse is a digital ecosystem based on blockchain technology. Visual components are provided by technologies such as VR and AR, while decentralized media allows for endless social engagement and business prospects. These environments are scalable, interoperable, and adaptable, and they combine novel technology and interaction models among their members on both an individual and organizational level.

Communications, money, gaming worlds, personal profiles, NFTs, and other processes and elements are all part of metaverses, which are digital 3D universes. The metaverse's promise is attributed to the freedom it provides; anyone in the metaverse can build, buy, and view NFTs to amass virtual land, join social communities, construct virtual identities, and play games, among other things. This diverse range of use cases opens up many possibilities for monetizing real-world and digital assets, with enterprises and individuals alike able to integrate into metaverse frameworks.

Future metaverses will bring together disparate online worlds, with NFTs allowing cross-chain interactions. To gain a better understanding of the metaverse.

How Will NFTs Impact The Metaverse?

In the metaverse, NFTs can disrupt the traditional social network paradigm of user contact, socializing, and transaction. Learn how NFTs may cause havoc in the digital world.

An Open And Fair Economy

Users and businesses can now transfer real-world assets and services into the metaverse, a decentralized virtual environment. Using novel gaming models with interoperable blockchain games is one method to bring more real-world assets into the metaverse.

One such option is the play-to-earn gaming concept, which engages and empowers blockchain game players. Players can participate in the in-game economies in the metaverse and earn incentives for the value they offer by relying on NFTs, basically earning while they play. In the metaverse, play-to-earn games are also fair since participants retain complete ownership of their assets rather than a single game entity, as is the case with most traditional games.

Suppose you're interested in participating in these in-game financial economies. In that case, Binance NFT's IGO launches provide a selection of in-game assets from gaming projects that players may gather and integrate into various gaming environments. Such in-game NFTs are in high demand, as evidenced by IGO debuts, where all NFTs were sold out on the first day. Axie Infinite (AXS), My Neighbor Alice (Alice), and many others are examples of successful play-to-earn games.

What is your metaverse financial strategy?

This year, that word has been all over the place. Facebook changed its name to Meta, regarded with skepticism and even outright scorn. NFT (short for non-fungible token) was named Collins Dictionary's word of the year, and such tokens are an important aspect of the expanding virtual universe. Before this version of the future arrived, everyone from gamers to developers to diplomats seemed eager to enter the metaverse.

Should you make a financial plan for the metaverse if it is the future? The mainstream advisor who urges you to spend $1.5 million on a few pieces of digital land will be rare. And it's still unclear how or even if the metaverse will take shape.

But, as we near the end of this year of meta-mania, it's a good idea to at least have a notion of how these new ways of working, playing, and investing can affect your finances. Or, you'll know what to say when someone in your family wonders, "What is the metaverse, anyway?" around the holidays.

Investments in Digital Assets: Virtual investing opportunities arise from a virtual universe. The value of digital land is skyrocketing. Republic Real Estate, a company that has collected money to buy troubled condos in the real world, created a fund focused on virtual land investors earlier this year. The company intends to buy packages from various online "metaverses" and turn them into virtual hotels, stores, and other purposes to boost their value among cryptocurrency enthusiasts.

NFT art has become one of the year's most popular digital assets. And Thomas Olsen, a partner at Bain & Co., has stated that he believes all assets would be tokenized in 20 or 30 years. "All equities, all bonds will be on a digital asset platform that the crypto experiment is building now,"

Online-Only Shopping and Experiences: Online purchasing will become even more complex if brands have their way. They've already made millions of dollars selling metaverse-exclusive apparel and accessories. It may sound foolish now, but if you do a lot of your job and play online, the way you look could come to matter a lot more. That's why it'll be crucial to keep track of how and why avatars of all races and genders are valued on the internet. Disparities are already beginning to emerge, with potentially catastrophic consequences.

Remote Work to the Extreme: In 1990, telling someone they needed to plan for the internet to destroy their industry could have seemed gloomy and even ridiculous, but not now. Is it possible that the same is true in the metaverse?

Remote work could become more permanent and immersed due to the meta modus operandi. Facebook, like the major kahuna of workplace technology, Microsoft, wants to transfer its vision of the office to the virtual world. Microsoft is currentl testing a version of its Teams chat and conferencing tool with digital avatars, which will be available in the first half of 2022. Customers will exchange Office files and functionality in the virtual world, such as PowerPoint decks.

Shifting Circumstances in the Real World: None of this implies that the real world will vanish any time soon. Firms will continue to adapt to Bitcoin, gaming, work, and everyday life merge in the real world.

For instance, we might see corporations relocate to real-world jurisdictions that are more sympathetic to the virtual world. That appears to be the case in Puerto Rico, where cheap taxes have attracted many crypto enthusiasts. If the bankers of the metaverse want to meet in San Juan, that's OK. However, I'll organize interviews with them at the beach rather than by phone. — Wells, Charlie

Who will control the metaverse

Who will pull the strings in what is being billed as the next internet iteration now that Facebook has turned to Meta? Eight digital marketing experts debate if decentralization will succeed or if big tech companies will maintain their walled gardens.

According to early investors, two essential components define a 'genuine' metaverse: decentralization and interoperability.

Decentralization spreads control and decision-making to a network rather than a single body pulling the strings. Consumers are in charge in this open, permissionless world, able to shape and choose the destiny of their experiences and be sovereign over their own identities and inventions. Decentralization is partly due to blockchain technology, which allows users to monitor the provenance and ownership of digital assets on a virtual ledger and may one day support self-sovereign identities.

Interoperability is enabled by storing data with individuals rather than with separate platforms, allowing users to simply teleport from one experience to the next using the same 'digital twin.'

This is in stark contrast to Web 2.0's closed ecosystems, in which platforms hold client data and digital assets are game-specific. Building 'walled gardens' around client data has enabled internet platforms to create powerful advertising engines that have propelled them to trillion-dollar valuations. In the so-called next iteration of the internet, are these behemoths willing to relinquish control over their most valuable commodity, customer data?

Mark Zuckerberg, a co-founder of Facebook who seeks to transform the social media firm into a "metaverse corporation," recently spoke about the difficulty of interoperability. He said the company needed to strike a compromise between "allowing research and interoperability but cutting down data as much as possible" during its third-quarter earnings call on October 25.

It's a worrying notion for those who want the metaverse to be based on consumer empowerment provided by decentralization, especially given how much money big tech is putting into it. Last week, Facebook rebranded its company portfolio to Meta to reflect its desire to establish the metaverse and has set aside "billions" to do it. While Zuckerberg has stated that the firm supports interoperability, the company's hardware strategy paints a different tale. The company's Oculus VR devices, for example, require a Facebook account to use.

We asked eight experts from across the marketing world for their perspectives on control and ownership in virtual reality in the fourth chapter of Campaign Asia-Pacific's series diving into the metaverse and how companies can prepare for it. Will big tech or consumers have the final say? Will there be several versions of the metaverse instead of a single, utopian, decentralized world? What value will platforms extract from their most valuable assets, and how will they protect them?

I predict the current walled gardens will focus all of their efforts on gaining control of the metaverse, which means it will cease to exist. And I anticipate that early-stage innovators and businesses will either resist or sell out to the walled gardens. Much will rely on whether those inventors are looking for a quick buck, a greater payoff later via an IPO, or the establishment of a new, decentralized internet 3.0. It could all come down to a handful of as-yet-unknown Lords of the Metaverse making personal life decisions during the epidemic. Make your wagers.

Tessa Conrad, head of innovation, TBWA Asia

It's still early days on this one, and it's a little difficult to wrap our heads around, I believe. The walled gardens we have now would not exist in a true metaverse, but those walls aren't going anywhere, so what does that mean for the metaverse? I believe that the current walled gardens will become more community-led. Isn't it true that businesses follow the money? And if money starts to flow away from their platforms due to the rise of lesser actors in the metaverse, they will pay heed.

With that in mind, I believe platforms will remain fairly walled but will open up more to cross-platform [in nature] integrations. I believe we will be able to port ourselves similarly with things like our currencies, digital assets, preferences, and avatars, similar to how our IDs are already routinely used across several platforms.

Consumers are more aware of their power than ever before. This is accomplished through their voice, personal communities, platform presence, and financial resources. They have the opportunity to leave at any time, and a flourishing competitive landscape means they will continue to have other options. As a result, we'll have to follow customers' lead, which I believe will be much more grassroots-driven. This is what we observe when we look at the current condition of DAOs (decentralized autonomous organizations). Voices are powerful on their own, but they are even more so when combined. Consumers are in charge of future advancements, investments, and new worlds because they band together to make decisions. Walled gardens must simply select if they want to be a part of that puzzle through integrations (or entirely opening up their platforms, which is improbable) or risk being left behind.

Michael Patent, founder, Culture Group

I don't think the largest platforms, such as Facebook, are ready to exist in decentralized or interoperable society, and I believe they'll attempt to create their own upgraded version of their world. Other platforms, whether gamified or music-driven, I believe recognize that their most valuable asset is their capacity to allow for fan development, user-generated content, and interoperability. The paradigm shift will be from "my biggest asset is my ability to hold on to this data and monetize it" to "my greatest asset is my ability to be distributed throughout the virtual universe."

Zoe Cocker, head of brand and Yahoo Creative Studios ANZ

I don't believe the metaverse will be 'owned' or 'controlled' by a single entity. The entire concept of Web 3.0 is based on interoperability, accessibility, and power decentralization. Facebook (or should I say Meta) is the latest in a long line of organizations to make bets on the future of the internet. The metaverse has grown exponentially, outpacing prior versions of the internet and the whole game industry. Take a look at Roblox or Fortnight, which have strong investment and user populations. Roblox was valued at $41.9 billion in March, with over 44.3 million users. While Meta will undoubtedly contribute to the metaverse in terms of attention, jobs, and research and development, I'm wary of it focusing solely on its ecology.

Instead, I'm betting on platforms like Decentraland, a truly decentralized virtual world that a single private corporation doesn't control. Decentraland, for example, hosted 'The Metaverse Festival' last week. Artists, musicians, NFT badges, digital wearables, creator stations and stalls, and much more will be on display. Everyone is welcome to join in and contribute. Yahoo organized an afterparty with Monkey Shoulder, a scotch whiskey brand, and featured performances by Krafty Kuts and A.Skillz on a branded stage with digital wearables. This is the version of the metaverse to which I subscribe: real collaboration-based innovation.

Laurent Thevenet, head of creative technology, Publicis Groupe Asia Pacific, Middle East & Africa

The metaverse is a broad term that encompasses a wide range of experiences. By focusing openly on it, Facebook (now Meta) joins a set of other ecosystems that have been in that sector for some time, such as Epic Games, Unity, and Roblox. When we examine it closely, it resembles the war between MacOS and Windows in the 1990s, or the more contemporary competition between Google, Facebook, and Apple to retain users within their various ecosystems. The metaverse is a new sort of predominantly immersive experience, necessitating the use of new hardware such as immersive headsets and glasses. This hardware will most likely only work in selected universes. The Oculus Quest is a fantastic example because it requires a Facebook account to use. This will keep these ecosystems separate from one another, with only a smattering of integration—much like we currently have in the non-metaverse.

According to Facebook, the metaverse is simply an immersive version of its current products. In light of the current social media concerns, it appears that the metaverse should serve as a blank canvas for all. A chance exists to place humans at the center of a new generation of experiences. A 2016 short film attempted to imagine what would happen if digital experiences were stacked on top of the actual world. It's impressive in terms of what technology can accomplish, but it's also horrifying in terms of what it could become. Immersive experiences must be approached with humanity in mind.

Emma Chiu, global director, Wunderman Thompson Intelligence

The metaverse is essentially the birth of a new tech-enabled society. It will be extremely difficult for a single firm to gain control because the people, or users, will revolt. Companies have been forced to open up so that some video games can be played on various devices from various manufacturers. The people are in charge of the metaverse. The metaverse would not exist if no one participated. So, while corporations compete for possession of the metaverse, individuals will not accept sole ownership.

Alex Wills, chief experience officer, The Mill

The incumbent tech corporations are expected to take similar paths to develop the most enticing regions inside the metaverse that allow for maximal and direct involvement and connection. This is the polar opposite of what the next transition should entail for many. However, just as there were new opportunities for new and existing players to create platforms and experiences that utilize the opportunities that decentralization and interoperability afford during the early days of social media and Facebook's platform.

Dick van Motman, founder and chair, UnVentures

"The state of being useful, profitable, or beneficial," according to the definition of utility, is a commonly used word in the tech sector. Platforms like Facebook began as a service but have since evolved into a so-called walled garden in which they assert control and make a lot of money.

The metaverse is built on the notion of interoperability and putting the user first, which runs as opposed to one-party control and, as a result, poses a threat to the existing large platforms. The instinct would be to create 'miniverses' that follow their rules or gobble up emerging metaverse players in the same way they've purchased Instagram and Oculus Rift. But, rather than continuously altering to provide meaningful utility, that would be putting form over function to protect what has been constructed. A simple rebranding highlights the ambition for continuing control into Meta.

In the end, there is only one permanent and central party in the metaverse: the customer. They'll choose and vote based on who can help them navigate the new universe easily. It will be owned by those who generate value and collaborate with users rather than controlling them. To put it another way, metaverse is the same as 'metacreator' and 'metaconsumer.'

Chapter 8:

MARKETING IN THE METAVERSE

Digital marketers must stay current with technological changes. Part of this is comprehending the metaverse and its full potential. Marketers need to realize that the metaverse isn't simply a fad; it appears to be here to stay and on its way to becoming the next big thing.

What strategies may marketers use to adapt as the metaverse grows?

First and foremost, marketers must remember the importance of millennials and Gen Zers as a target demographic. Some sorts of metaverses, such as games like Roblox and technologies like VR, are also popular among these generations. Let's look at how marketing can be done in the metaverse with that in mind.

Parallel metaverse marketing within real-life marketing

Create marketing experiences that connect with real-life events or are similar to what your company already does in the real world. In June, for example, AB InBev's beer brand Stella Artois collaborated with Zed Run to create a Tamagotchi-inspired Kentucky Derby experience. They did so because Stella Artois, a brand of AB InBev, is known for supporting sporting events, particularly horse racing. As a result, developing an online platform where non-fungible token (NFT) horses may be sold, raced, and bred appears to be a natural next step for them.

Immersive experience is key

In the metaverse, you can sell virtual advertising. Bidstack, a video game ad tech company, shifted from real-world outdoor advertising to virtual billboard advertising.

However, virtual billboards aren't the only option. Because metaverses are engaging and immersive by nature, it's ideal to capitalize on this by providing a similarly immersive experience with your commercials and marketing efforts. Instead of merely posting advertising, offer branded installations and events users may interact with.

We've seen early adopters provide immersive experiences to their consumers, such as a Lil Nas X performance in Roblox, Gucci Garden experience visits, and Warner Bros.' marketing of In the Heights with a virtual reproduction of the Washington Heights neighborhood. Collaborations with the Roblox metaverse and other metaverses have recently shown new revenue sources for brands.

Make collectibles available

People enjoy collecting stuff, and the metaverse provides them with yet another platform to do so. You can replicate the experience in the metaverse by providing assets or limited-edition items that can only be obtained in the metaverse.

The Collector's Room, for example, is available in the Gucci Garden Roblox experience. In the metaverse, it allows users to gather limited-edition Gucci products. Gucci made a total of 286,000,000 Robux from the game's initial sales of collectible products.

Engage with existing communities

The public generally dislikes advertising. As businesses try to break into the metaverse, they mustn't offend those already there. You'll also need the favorable feedback of these users because you'll be marketing to them.

Remember that you can't simply enter a new platform without considering the new format. When businesses collaborate with members of the Roblox developer community to create things and experiences, for example, they gain more traction. Similarly, when O2 put on a Fortnite performance, they teamed up with developers who were already experts on the game.

Consider this a form of influencer marketing. Community members become key aspects of the execution of your campaigns since user-generated content is important.

Continuously experiment

Marketers are living in an exciting moment. While some guiding principles can help marketers determine what techniques and methods to use, the metaverse is still a relatively young platform with plenty of potential for experimentation. Best practices are still being defined, and paradigms are still being developed in their entirety. This provides marketers a lot of leeways to explore new things and be unique in their approaches.

Other Exceptional Metaverse Cases

• Dimension Studio's experimentation with metaverses for fashion labels generated $6.5 million in sales. They created a virtual production set-up that allows users to go onto a platform, get scanned by 106 cameras, and then be placed into virtual worlds to try on clothes and other items. They are well recognized for Balenciaga's Autumn/Winter 2021 Afterworld game.

• Grand Theft Auto V, an open-world sandbox game, included dress options similar to those worn by Hong Kong demonstrators. Many artists have been reusing virtual worlds for political expression, and Hong Kong demonstrators could take their conflict in the real world into the metaverse.

• Houzz, a home decor website, allows users to create digital photo collections of their furniture and other household objects. Houzz makes money every time someone uses their service to buy something. They developed a 3D viewer in 2017 that allows users to view products in 3D directly through a camera and visually integrates them into their physical area.

• Google Maps demonstrated an augmented reality tool for its walking directions. This feature provides users with precise visual directions and arrows to help them navigate their way to their destinations. Simply point the user's camera in the direction they require guidance, and the AR function will guide them on the right path.

Chapter 9:

TOP METAVERSE INVESTMENTS TO SKYROCKET

Metaverse stocks have become one of the most popular Wall Street trends. The metaverse space is gradually emerging from sci-fi literature and movies to become a reality, thanks to significant advances in virtual reality technology and computational capacity.

In the metaverse, which consists of digital online environments, people may live, work, and play. It's a virtual environment that anybody can share thanks to the merging of virtual and physical reality.

Meta Platforms (NASDAQ: FB) In late October, when CEO Mark Zuckerberg unveiled the company's new name, aimed to emphasize its focus on the metaverse, it drew the attention of investors. "The defining quality of the metaverse will be a sense of presence — as if you are right there with another person or in another place,"

Zuckerberg stated. Our role in this journey is to speed up the development of the foundational technologies, social platforms, and creative tools that will bring the metaverse to life, as well as to weave these technologies together through our social media apps."

Companies increasingly focus on developing this technology and expanding the metaverse's boundaries. Bloomberg Intelligence says the metaverse business might be worth $800 billion by 2024.

Investors are scrambling to find safe bets on the arrival of this game-changing technology. In light of such upside potential, I'll go through seven metaverse stocks to buy now that have promising growth prospects.

With that in mind, here are seven metaverse stocks that could pay off handsomely in 2022:

Fastly (NYSE: FSLY)

Immersion (NASDAQ:IMMR)

Matterport (NASDAQ:MTTR)

Meta Platforms

Roblox (NYSE: RBLX)

Roundhill Ball Metaverse ETF (NYSEARCA: META)

Unity Software (NYSE: U)

Metaverse Stocks: Fastly (FSLY)

52-week range: $33.87 – $122.75

The company is based in San Francisco, California. According to Cloudflare, Fastly runs a real-time content delivery network (CDN), which is defined as "a geographically distributed group of servers that work together to offer fast delivery of Internet content" (NYSE: NET). Fastly provides cloud services in delivery, security, compute, and performance.

On Nov. 3, management released its third-quarter results. Year-over-year (YOY) revenue increased by 23% to $87 million. In the prior-year quarter, the company lost $56 million, or 48 cents per diluted share, compared to $24 million, or 22 cents per diluted share. Cash and equivalents totaled $282 million at the end of the quarter.

Fastly provides edge computing infrastructure-as-a-service (IaaS), which brings servers and equipment closer to the point where data is generated. Fastly is well-positioned to gain from the metaverse because it requires a large quantity of data transfer to generate a virtual world in real-time. Its infrastructure helps to reduce decentralization's lag time and latency, and it can transmit 167 gigabytes of data per second across multiple nations.

According to a new industry research analysis, edge computing is anticipated to be valued at roughly $87 billion by 2026, with a compound annual growth rate (CAGR) of 19%. Investors can buy FSLY stock at a reasonable price because of its high growth potential. It's hovering at $49 right now, down 45 percent year to date (YTD). Fastly's stock is trading at 17.1 times trailing revenue, down almost 60% from its peak in late January.

Immersion (IMMR)

52-week range: $6.41 – $16.64

The company is based in San Jose, California. Immersion is a pioneer in the field of haptics or touches feedback. The company's cutting-edge technology interacts with users' tactile senses. Mobility, gaming, automotive, and consumer electronics all employ its devices.

On November 3, Immersion revealed its third-quarter results. Total revenue fell 5% year over year to $7.2 million, from $7.6 million the previous quarter. Non-

GAAP net income, on the other hand, grew 14 percent year over year to $4.7 million, or 15 cents per diluted share, up from $4.1 million the previous quarter.

Cash and short-term marketable securities totaled $119 million at the end of the quarter. Because more than 90% of sales are recurring, the company has a steady cash flow. It is also debt-free.

With its DualSense haptic controllers used by Sony's (NYSE: SONY) PlayStation 5, Immersion cemented its position as a leader in haptic technology. However, the mobility business continues to generate the majority of the company's revenue.

Titan Haptics, based in Canada, signed an arrangement with the company in August. It will now make its haptic patent licenses accessible to mobile phones and wearable OEMs who use TITAN actuators, which are devices that "create motion by translating energy and signals going into the system."

Since early November, the shares of IMMR have dropped by more than 20%. It is currently trading just around $7 per share, down 40% year to date. Shares are currently trading at 5.7 times trailing sales; therefore, investors should consider purchasing now.

Metaverse Stocks: Matterport (MTTR)

52-week range: $10.45 – $28

The company is based in Sunnyvale, California. Matterport is a firm that digitizes and indexes the world's space data. Spatial data analytics is becoming increasingly significant in business. On their website, Aspectum, a geospatial intelligence firm, offers more information:

"Location is one thing that all data sets have in common. And it is this feature that enables companies and entities to assemble data points on spatial analysis maps in a pleasing manner."

Matterport began operations in 2011 and went public in July through a special purpose acquisition company (SPAC). Individuals can use its 3D data platform to turn an area into a precise and immersive digital twin, or "digital copy of a real-world place or thing."

Digital twins are commonly used in the construction and real estate industries. Matterport, for example, allows real estate companies to create digital twins of their structures. Prospective buyers or tenants can then take a virtual tour of the property from the convenience of their own homes.

In addition, Matterport for Mobile was just released, allowing 3D capture to be done on mobile devices for free.

The third-quarter results were released on November 3 by management. Revenue grew 10% year over year to $27.7 million. The non-GAAP net loss was $14 million, or 6 cents per diluted share, compared to a non-GAAP net income of $1.5 million, or 1 cent per diluted share, the year before. Cash and equivalents were $149 million at the end of the quarter.

Matterport makes money by selling the tools needed to work in virtual environments. Matterport's platform received over 6.2 million digital twins during the third quarter. Total members climbed by 116% year over year, while subscription revenue increased 36%.

As a newbie to Wall Street, Matterport may appear to be a high-risk investment. However, the stock's huge upside potential may be worth investigating further.

Annual revenue is expected to increase dramatically in 2022 due to its significant first-mover advantage.

The stock of MTTR is currently trading at approximately $28, up more than 140 percent in the last six months. The stock is currently trading at 26 times its book value. A possible fall approaching $20 could be a better entry point for interested readers.

Meta Platforms (FB)

52-week range: $244.61 – $384.33

Meta Platforms (formerly known as Facebook) has become one of the most well-known digital advertising companies globally, thanks to its social media platforms and apps. And, as we've already discussed, it has big plans to dominate the metaverse.

On October 25, Meta Platforms released its third-quarter results. Revenue increased by 35% year over year to $29 billion. In the previous quarter, it earned $9.2 billion in net income, or $3.22 per diluted share, compared to $7.9 billion, or $2.71 per diluted share. Cash and equivalents totaled $58 billion at the end of the quarter.

"We made good progress this quarter, and our community continues to grow," Zuckerberg said of the measures. I'm pleased about our plans, particularly those related to creators, commerce, and assisting in the development of the metaverse."

Meta Platforms launched horizon Workrooms in August. Horizon Workrooms allows users to engage in virtual reality (VR) meetings using digital avatars via VR goggles. The company also unveiled a pair of smart glasses that can be used to take images, videos, or make phone calls.

Facebook stock appears to be one of the safest bets in the metaverse with strong fundamentals. Currently, it is trading about $340, representing a nearly 25% year-to-date gain. At 23 times forward earnings and 8.7 times revenue, shares appear to be less expensive than they were a few months ago.

Metaverse Stocks: Roblox (RBLX)

52-week range: $60.50 – $119

The company is based in San Mateo, California. Roblox is a prominent online entertainment platform where individuals may explore and create 3D experiences created by others. Roblox is popular among players under 18 years old, with 48 million average daily active users as of August.

According to analysts, Roblox's present platform is as near to a social metaverse as it gets for the time being. New content is constantly being created by third-party developers to be included in existing games.

On November 8, Roblox released its third-quarter earnings. Sales increased 102 percent year over year to $509 million, excluding deferred revenue. In the previous quarter, the company's net loss increased to $74 million, or 13 cents per diluted share, from $48.6 million, or 26 cents per diluted share. The company's free cash flow improved by 7% year over year to $170.6 million. Cash and equivalents were $1.9 billion at the end of the quarter.

"We're thrilled that players of all ages from all over the world choose to spend over 11 billion hours on Roblox during the third quarter," CEO David Baszucki said after the news. We're pleased to inform you that the developer community made more than $130 million in the first quarter and is on track to make well over $500 million this year."

After the company released its third-quarter earnings on Nov. 9, RBLX stock soared by more than 40%. The stock reached a fresh all-time high of $119 today. A further decrease below $90 would be a better entry point for interested readers.

Roundhill Ball Metaverse ETF (META)

52-Week Range: $13.75 – $16.70

Expense ratio: 0.75% per year

The company is based in San Mateo, California. Roblox is a prominent online entertainment platform where individuals may explore and create 3D experiences created by others. Roblox is popular among players under 18 years old, with 48 million average daily active users as of August.

According to analysts, Roblox's present platform is as near to a social metaverse as it gets for the time being. New content is constantly being created by third-party developers to be included in existing games.

On November 8, Roblox released its third-quarter earnings. Sales increased 102 percent year over year to $509 million, excluding deferred revenue. In the previous quarter, the company's net loss increased to $74 million, or 13 cents per diluted share, from $48.6 million, or 26 cents per diluted share. The company's free cash flow improved by 7% year over year to $170.6 million. Cash and equivalents were $1.9 billion at the end of the quarter.

"We're thrilled that players of all ages from all over the world choose to spend over 11 billion hours on Roblox during the third quarter," CEO David Baszucki said after the news. We're pleased to inform you that the developer community made more than $130 million in the first quarter and is on track to make well over $500 million this year."

After the company released its third-quarter earnings on Nov. 9, RBLX stock soared by more than 40%. The stock reached a fresh all-time high of $119 today. A further decrease below $90 would be a better entry point for interested readers.

Metaverse Stocks: Unity Software (U)

52-week range: $76 – $207

Unity Software is a game development platform that enables game developers to produce and commercialize real-time 3D content for mobile phones, tablets, consoles, PCs, and virtual reality headsets.

On November 9, the company's third-quarter results were revealed. Revenue grew by 43% year over year to $286 million. In the previous quarter, the non-GAAP loss increased to $12.1 million, or 6 cents per diluted share, from $8.4 million, or 9 cents per diluted share. The company's free cash flow was $34 million. Cash and equivalents totaled $766 million at the end of the quarter.

"Innovation in data science, vertical expansion, and making substantial progress in providing RT3D technology and tools to as many creators and artists as possible drove Unity's outstanding performance this quarter," said CEO John Riccitiello.

Unity's technology is used by almost every major player in the worldwide video game industry. Unity's platform has created 71% of the top 1,000 mobile games. If you want to bet on the gamification of the metaverse, U stock is a good place to start.

Unity Gaming Services is a framework that allows developers to produce 2D and 3D content for augmented reality (AR) and virtual reality (VR) devices. In addition, Unity announced a collaboration with Tripolygon, a metaverse 3D modeling service.

It shouldn't be long before Unity turns a profit as it expands into areas other than video games. Industrial applications, film, animation, and engineering projects increasingly use the platform.

Chapter 10:

HOW METAVERSE IS EVOLVING DIGITAL WORLD?

Outsiders frequently mix up Metaverse and Virtual Reality. They believe Metaverse is a new form of virtual reality technology. Some people believe it is the internet's future. Even if these notions are correct, the digital world is evolving. Although it may appear to be science fiction, Metaverse digitally combines personal and business life in a way that is similar to our physical world. However, you may be wondering why this technology is capturing people's interest and why they are investing so heavily in the digital world.

Unlike virtual reality (VR) technology, which we utilize in video games, Metaverse incorporates all potential activities. You can do everything online, from hanging out with pals to going to the movies, playing tennis, and going to concerts. Take a closer look at how Metaverse will transform our world:

1. Economic Changes

Metaverse will alter the way we do business in the future. It has an impact on how people think when they buy things. As a result, businesses will perform more market research in order to better understand their customers' behavior. The experience of buying things in a physical store is not the same as what Metaverse provides. As a result, every company must upgrade its operations. Customer contacts will undoubtedly be handled by robots and virtual assistants. For data analysis, these bots will be equipped with powerful computing equipment.

2. Cultural Changes

Metaverse will affect cultural standards since it links people from many ethnic backgrounds. People in the Metaverse will have connections and friendships just like they do in the physical world. They do, however, engage through holograms and self-contained NPCs. The Metaverse will have an impact on the corporate world and will bring customers together in 3D. They won't be able to communicate with marketing people, but they will be able to communicate with bots to get answers to their questions.

3. Shopping Experience

In comparison to physical purchasing, the Metaverse shopping experience is unique. In the Metaverse, virtual real estate, avatar skins, and virtual fashion have great value. People will also invest in enterprises and properties that do not exist physically. Because people will use avatars to represent themselves, the fashion industry will focus on designing clothing for the characters. People would also look for virtual designer clothes and mansions to invest in.4. Entertainment Industry

In the Metaverse, virtual concerts, seminars, and gatherings will be commonplace. Celebrities and brands will use the virtual world to interact with their fans. We now use technology to make purchases and play games. People, on the other hand, would virtually spend time with their pals at restaurants, events, and cafés. Wendy's, for example, is experimenting with putting their restaurant in the Metaverse so that consumers may engage with their friends there. Ariana Grande's concert in

Fortnite Metaverse on August 7, 2021 is another example of a Metaverse entertainment event.

THE EVOLUTION OF INTERNET 3.0 WITH METAVERSE

For the time being, metaverse appears to be more of a branding exercise, an attempt to bring together pieces that are already forming online. It is possible that it will radically revolutionize consumer and business behavior if it comes to fruition as ambitiously as anticipated.

Following Mark Zuckerberg's rebranding of Facebook to Meta, the 'Metaverse' has become a popular issue, but what precisely does this mean? Everything you do on the modern internet experience is currently two-dimensional, i.e. the browse and scroll functions. The Metaverse is a three-dimensional, immersive next-generation version of the internet that is mostly created using augmented reality and virtual reality technology.

For some, though, this may not be a shocking surprise; the concept of a virtual world has been around us for several years through a variety of platforms.

Every day, millions of individuals spend hours in virtual social places such as Roblox and Fortnite. Gucci, the luxury fashion house, said in March that they will be selling a pair of virtual-only sneakers for £8.99, while Puma, Reebok, and Farfetch all have similar online-only collections.

This paradigm was pioneered by augmented reality apps like Pokémon Go, which debuted in 2016. Snapchat is one of the best-case instances of how the metaverse is already infiltrating the daily lives of millions of people without them noticing it. Their unique filters enable marketers to connect with customers on a more personal level through highly interactive content.

Entrepreneurs are constructing an alternative monetary system utilizing blockchain technology, buying and selling virtual real-estate assets and digital currencies, and the metaverse has made an appearance in financial institutions as well.

Players can acquire, train, and breed animals that are registered on the Ethereum blockchain in blockchain-based games like Axie Infinity. These digital options have inspired a younger population to look to the metaverse as a viable place to create their fortunes, particularly in the last several years.

As a result of Covid-19, there has been a significant movement in the digital world, particularly when it comes to working remotely. Despite initial fears, the global epidemic has provided limitless chances for growth, collaboration, and creativity.

For both individuals and employers, the future of work appears to be more streamlined. People in this world can customize their avatars (virtual representations of themselves) and use them to visit a meeting room from the comfort of their own homes. On the notion of launching Mesh in Microsoft Teams, Microsoft CEO Satya Nadella said people can communicate on a virtual whiteboard or walk around a virtual 3D model of a car they're developing in that room.

A metaverse will also allow retail behemoths to provide more dynamic in-store experiences. Virtual reality and augmented reality headsets will allow customers to try on things in the store, regardless of whether they are in stock or not. This virtual environment has the promise of allowing enormous overlap between our digital and physical lives in terms of money, productivity, shopping, and enjoyment.

With cryptocurrencies and non-fungible tokens (NFTs) making a genuine influence in global markets, interest in a deeper digital world has exploded. However, suppose the metaverse is simply an extension of the internet that we presently have. In that case, it's also vital to consider the plethora of issues that we have yet to address in our current online presence, such as catfishing, harassment, cybercrime, hacking, and hate speech.

For the time being, metaverse appears to be more of a branding exercise, an attempt to bring together pieces already forming online. It's possible that if it comes to completion as ambitiously as intended, it will revolutionize consumer and business behavior.

Chapter 11:

METAVERSE: THE EVOLUTION OF A NOVEL TECHNOLOGY AND WHAT IT MEANS FOR THE FUTURE

The Metaverse can further disrupt numerous businesses by delivering virtual reality (VR)-based wearables that transfer individuals to another virtual world from the comfort of their homes.

Suppose the previous century was defined by mass production and the introduction of the Internet. In that case, the twenty-first century may be known for the invention and expansion of the virtual world, or Metaverse, which offers more interactive, collaborative, and immersive than the Internet.

Despite the promises made by many entrepreneurs experimenting in this field, it has become abundantly evident that Blockchain technology will underlie the

Metaverse and help establish a sustainable environment for all participants. While it is reasonable to believe that the Metaverse will influence traditional jobs or activities that are fairly commonplace now, its impact on society and how humans interact with one another will be significant.

When the COVID-19 outbreak swept the globe, damaging economies, the Internet and the resulting Work from Home (WFH) technology aids played a critical role in keeping businesses afloat, and in some instances, rapidly expanding. As a result of the pandemic, certain industries, like education, have seen substantial changes and are now more technology-intensive.

By supplying virtual reality (VR)-based wearables that allow users to experience an alternate virtual world without leaving their homes, the Metaverse can potentially disrupt existing businesses further. People would be able to communicate without having to travel long distances, breathe polluted air, or dress up for different occasions. Children will study a range of courses and modules at their own pace, expanding their horizons beyond what traditional syllabi provide.

After-work activities such as watching movies or socializing with friends would be available in the virtual world without the difficulties of the actual world.

Outside of the United States and Canada, Together Labs' IMVU platform will offer VCORE, an ERC-20 token that rewards active, global gamers, producers, and earners across the metaverse. With the launch of a new token in 2022, VCORE should give its users access to a new sort of economy in which everyone may contribute to the growth of the metaverse.

"The purpose of our inaugural presale was to interact with and garner interest from the top strategic crypto and metaverse purchasers who are well-versed in our field," stated John Burris, Together Labs' Chief Strategy and Blockchain Officer. "When we release VCORE next year, we will have a powerful one-two punch with our original token, VCOIN, a globally transferable fiat-backed token, now VCORE to drive the next generation Metaverse economy."

The success of the metaverse, like any ecosystem, will be determined by how simple it is for individuals to transact in it. This is where cryptocurrencies come in, and several projects that utilize them to facilitate real-world and digital transactions have already set the ball moving. Due to the capacity to readily convert fiat currency to cryptocurrencies, people will shift between the real world and the Metaverse with amazing ease.

Using crypto tokens provided by corporations enabling these virtual connections, consumers will be able to buy digital avatars, virtual land, and even throw a party for loved ones. Artists will perform in the Metaverse, receive payment in crypto, and then swap their winnings for physical goods. The Metaverse's growth will enhance the amount of wealth that may be unlocked, perhaps resulting in a rapid global economic expansion.

"Not only has Mint Gold Dust built an NFT platform, but also a whole complementary ecosystem where an artist may mint their masterpieces, which we call "Gold Dust," and Geo Drop-in AR form all over the world," says Kelly LeValley Hunt, CEO of Mint Gold Dust. A collector may link their wallet to their collection and geo-drop it anywhere over the world to show it off. We think of NFTs for physical items in the Phygital Space as important for wearables, but there's a new notion called

ARTourism, in which a tour guide can use a GeoDropped NFT to teach you about architecture, art, and even history, so it's no longer just about wearables. It's about reality and virtual reality's progress, as well as technology breakthroughs and education."

According to Dominic Ryder, CEO of vEmpire, the metaverse has become the inevitable development for how people connect online, and the possibilities are unlimited — There's the Sandbox, which is for gamers and creative minds who want to build experiences; there's also Decentraland, which is becoming a hub for all kinds of events. "Then there's Axie Infinity and Starl, which are two completely different models and platforms, yet equally thriving in that digital space. I believe the pandemic has accelerated this progression, as almost everyone used to working in an office has been forced to adapt. It will only be a matter of time until those folks spend more time outside of work in the metaverse," Ryder predicts.

An embryonic form of the Metaverse exists today, with digital products such as Non-Fungible Tokens (NFTs) that mirror popular art and digital artifacts drawing both investors and crypto fans. With major players like Facebook, or Meta as it's currently known, entering this space and boldly signaling that the Metaverse is the new future, it'll only be a matter of time before other entities follow suit, resulting in a massive expansion of the Metaverse's boundaries and unlocking enormous amounts of value previously unknown to investors and consumers.

CONCLUSION

Without a question, the Metaverse will have huge ramifications in our society. It will alter the way we communicate, market, and brand ourselves. In addition, this ground-breaking technology will present new opportunities and difficulties. The metaverse has the potential to unleash great creativity and expand our economic, entertainment, and cultural horizons.